The Formula We Call Life

Understanding comes through seeing the whole picture

This is an intense book totally written from the heart of the author. The text is open to all readers regardless of their faith or conviction, and opens an understanding of spiritualism by the fact that the Author is highly knowledgeable on the subject. This book deserves to be on anyone's bookshelf, and will stand confidently amongst other books of a similar genre

Contents

The Formula We Call Life 1
    Introduction 3
        God's Words 3
Section One 10
    Chapter One: Optimise Your Life 10
    Chapter Two: Understanding God 43
    Chapter Three: Spirit Realms and Forces 59
    Chapter Four: Beyond Earth 87
    Chapter 5: Earth's Beginnings 113
    Chapter Six: Understanding the Planet's Needs ... 122
    Chapter Seven: Healing, Balancing Life 153
    So, the question is: 158
Section Two 177
    Developing and Shaping Your Life 177
Section 3: 233
    Simply Life Changing Tools and Prayers 233
        Personal Prayers 250
Natural 256

Introduction

On the 26th January 2023, I was sitting and checking a page from this book when I was aware of God's Presence. I knew immediately that it was to be the beginning of my Introduction for my book.

God's Words

We come to this life with such unique beginnings and that is the start of a learning time; a time of adjustment, growth, and value to achieve a wisdom that will add to that which we already possess.

We may be assertive or withdrawn, proud or humble, wise, or ignorant, but each journey brings a value to our lives that cannot be altered except by God.

His Wisdom and His Value hold and bring us exceptional quality, whether we are whole or disabled.

It's God's Will that guides us and brings torment, cruelty or upset if that is necessary, or if we wish for goodness and the solitude, that brings growth.

If we wish for goodness, we will hope and become a person of goodness, but so many times we ask for the upset that brings more upset.

Introducing The Formula

So often we ask, 'What's life about? Why are we here?'

If you follow science's conclusion, it clearly shows you how life developed, and how the human race has evolved to the level of intelligence that it now possesses. No argument there.

But it doesn't explain why, and surely that's just as important.

I've always believed that there's a purpose to my being here. Yet science fails to shine a light on the reason, and as each person on this planet is making their own journey on Earth, without that information it's inconclusive.

So, let's each ask the questions now...
Why am I here at this time?
Why am I living this type of life?
Why is life so challenging?
Then there are questions about the planet…

Is its existence just random? Did it happen for no particular reason, and then, over time humankind evolved?

Surely, of all things, logic should tell us that there was a need for all of that to occur, because it would be a waste of valuable experience if this life leads us to nothing more, and we're all here facing the challenges of life for no particular reason. That wouldn't make sense; and, if there's one section of humanity that needs things to make sense, it's the scientists.

Some people do believe that there is nothing to believe in, and that what we have now is as good as it gets. They deduce that this is it. In other words, a random life followed by the finality of death.

But isn't life worth more than that? Aren't I? Aren't you?

In this book you'll find answers to many questions as well as those you haven't yet asked.

Speaking Personally**,** I've never doubted that there's a God. I just couldn't take in the concept of a Spirit Being that was Omnipotent, and so I doubted that with all the work He had to do, that He would even know who I was.

'Frances Munro? Never heard of her!'
How wrong could I be!

Religion's versions of God left me with more questions than answers, but it was all I had when I was young, and as life was demanding enough on its own, I didn't spend much time contemplating the Creator.

So, it was some years later that my life turned around, and God and the whole life process became an important focus.

When you do focus, you discover that beneath the façade of material-based values created over the centuries by mankind, there are also core values and goals that are far more precious. They do affect your life on Earth, your future development within the Universe, and even the life of this planet.

To know that you have the ability to enhance or deplete the health of your planetary home should make you realise the responsibility everyone holds on Earth. But even more than that, because the positive and negative energies that you contribute during your life on the planet ultimately affects the overall power of the Galaxy and beyond. Can you really afford to treat Earth as something you would use and then throw away. Surely it deserves better from the Human Race.

Through the work I'm doing now, life has become clearer to me, I've received answers I understand, and life has taken on more meaning.

So, if we are to face together the serious challenges of saving our planet, achieving crucial goals, and creating a truly powerful future for ourselves and the world around us, we need to be well equipped. And who better to do that for us than God?

Let me say now, 'God is not an optional extra to life. *GOD IS INTEGRAL TO LIFE.*'

Need convincing? Just give me your open mind and I'll bring you the information that I possess.

Your time on Earth is only a tiny part of your overall life, and it has the makings of a valuable experience, but only you can make that happen.

It's a fascinating and powerful picture, so stay with me for this journey of words, and let it change your perspective on life and God as it has mine. Because Creation isn't random. It has a purpose. And the intricacies of life cannot be based on a simple 'use and dispose' formula.

With the intervention of science and technology, there's been a swing to developing the brain's logic, and that's fine if it's balanced with soul understanding, but that hasn't happened, and logic alone cannot supply the full picture. So, when your soul's message is 'unheard', your life inevitably adopts a different path, and its true purpose can be lost. Multiply that with everyone throughout the world, and suddenly the planet is in trouble.

As difficult as the experience may sometimes be, you and I are here to face challenges that each of us chose long ago, while we were still simply a spirit/ soul on our eternal journey of development.

If you ask 'why?' the answer is that if you develop your particular skills here on Earth, you're able not only to help the world to grow in a positive way, but also aid your own future spiritual development.

Strange as it may seem, you **have** chosen some painful bits, because it's valuable to you on a journey that doesn't end here at the closing of your Earthly life.

Accept that and you'll begin to see a wider picture.

In 'The Formula We Call Life', I want to use the information I've been given to take you on a journey of understanding exactly what your time here means, how valuable it is, and how the planning of it *did* involve God long before the physical act that brought your birth parents into the equation.

I also want to show you, through the information that I've been given by immensely powerful spirit beings, including God, why we must act urgently to save our planet, and divert our world from its damaging course to a safer one, where we can build peace and trust, the foundation for a more fulfilling life.

I will also share with you details about the spirit team that works to fulfil the needs of God. These powerful spirit beings are integral to our lives as they help us to find and fulfil our true purpose; but many work unnoticed in the background, so we simply talk to God to access that help.

I shall briefly explain the roles of archangels, angels, elementals, and spirit guides that work to help us balance our lives better and achieve the most from them. It's also important that I unravel any confusion about the agents of evil, and then explain Satan's true role.

I need you to understand the various elements of your life formula, so that you can empower areas of it to raise your understanding to new spiritual heights. That can help you both here, and when you return home to re-join that long path of learning within the Spirit Realms; for the decisions you take now, and later in spirit will aid you towards further development within the Realms. Alternatively, it may bring you back for another life on this planet or take you on a new experience somewhere else within the Galaxy. The opportunities are there for you.

So, let's look beyond this planet and let me open your eyes, and your understanding to the amazing life within this world, and to the powerful beings that maintain balance within this Universe and others too. Because if you close your mind to areas outside Planet Earth, you'll only see a small part of the picture, and yet we all have a responsibility, as well as a vital part to play, within our Galaxy and beyond.

I must emphasise how important it is that we now work together to heal our planet; because we only have a limited time to achieve this. But along with that, I must also introduce you to those who are unseen but are already helping us to repair the damage, in order to bring back a true balance within Earth's core.

The second part of this book focuses on simple exercises and routines that will help to change your life.

Piece by piece, they can guide you to focus better and learn about God-given and *natural* helpers such as colour, crystals, prayer, nature and more.

Your day-to-day life offers a mix of situations both good and problematic. But once you know how to knock down any thorny barriers of negativity and focus on positive solutions, your life will become more rewarding, and you'll learn to expect more from each day, as well as from yourself.

I've had many of my own experiences and lessons, and I'll share some of these with you.

Some subjects within this book may at first challenge your own understanding and beliefs but give them space and they'll sit well with you, because when you knock down any barriers pre-set by some religious teaching, atheism, and areas of science they fit together; and when you no longer have to clamber over obstacles, your path becomes easier, and you're able to see how you can empower your journey. You even develop a hunger to learn, and as you do, you understand better how you can apply your life in a positive and powerful way. I know because I've been there.

So often we see glimpses of the real life, but not the complete picture. It's like pieces of a jigsaw. We have them but where do they fit, and what links them?

Speaking Personally, when I began my own journey, I had no idea where it would take me, but just as they said in the film, 'Matrix' I needed to see how far down the rabbit hole went.

For over 25 years I've been blessed with the skill to receive information from powerful spirit communicators and guides, and they've been generous with their knowledge throughout. They've answered my questions, and I hope that here they'll answer some of yours too. After all, they know that it's essential that we understand the many changes now happening in our world that will affect our future as a race.

So, with communicating Spirit Guides such as White Cloud, Esquaygo, Abuhindra, Jesus, and even God Himself I have spent many years preparing for this stage with the Powers that work for the future of Humanity and Planet Earth.

You see, long ago the Powers within the Spirit Realms recognised the dangerous path that humanity was creating for itself. It saw a young planet growing prematurely old and weak, through the negative forces thrust upon it by so many nations that have lost their concern for the living. With our wars, chemicals, and rubbish we're killing the very planet we call home, and without help and a willingness to change, we cannot achieve our own development for our future in the Realms, or save what should be to us, a cherished world.

So, it's time to play our part and that's the reason for this book. It may play a small supportive part, or a bigger one. For me it's simply drawing together the powerful information given to me by God and my spirit guides and sharing it with you. It's fascinating, it's powerful, and at last it builds a picture that enables us to achieve what we came to this life to do.

My own life has developed into an adventure with a purpose, and I'm still in the middle of it. So please join me, and we'll get started.

As you step off on this journey

The subject of God is a vital part of this book. In fact, God is integral to our life and the future of this planet. I'll explain more about that later. Meanwhile, although I respect the many other Names that refer to this Being, in this book, I'll keep only to this one. My own feeling is of a Fatherly Energy, so you'll notice that I also use the words, 'He' and 'Him'. Please don't let it be a barrier. Just use the Name you're comfortable with.

Also, instead of referring to Heaven and Hell, I'll be talking about the Spirit Realms, but you'll understand more when I describe it in more detail. So let's get going.

Section One

Chapter One: Optimise Your Life

What Is A Human Life?

I've been curious about life since I was a child, but I had no siblings, and among adults you were supposed to be seen and not heard, so I worked out things the best I could on my own. Google hadn't been invented, and I thought everyone saw scenes play out when they shut their eyes.

Like every other astute person on Earth, I'm still learning every day, but over the past twenty six years, I've experienced a rich journey with valuable spirit teachers and amazing lessons, so I also have much to share.

My mother ensured that I had a Christian upbringing, but later I questioned things in the Bible, as well as the attitude and dogma of many religions and their representatives.

So, I shed the constrictive religious labels, and took from them only that which sat right with my soul. In their place I have created my own valuable journey with God, and that has been enriching, introducing me to understanding and ability I didn't know I was capable of.

If, along the way I use words that smack of religion, it's only because I'm not going to create a whole new vocabulary in order to avoid familiar terms. After all, we're here to break down barriers, not build new ones.

I started my adult life as a racing and sports car mechanic so I may also throw in some old engineering terms.

We're all here on our own unique journeys, and this is the start of understanding your own, and how you can strengthen it with God's help.

Knowledge is empowering, but only when you accept the full picture. So, here we're going to tackle as many areas as we can of what life on Earth represents, because there's so much more to it than we see with our eyes.

Of course, there isn't one formula that fits every being on the planet. But there *is* a single formula that describes the **basis** of a human life on Earth. So where do you stand on this Life Map and what are the basic materials that construct this complicated human frame?

The formula for *every* person on Earth is a Human body + Human brain + Soul/ Spirit. Basically, you could call it a human construction with an eternal engine (your soul).

Those, who **don't** accept the existence of God, don't actually lack any of the qualities that offer a connection with God. They simply choose to use nothing but the basic energy that the soul delivers. That's still power delivered by God, but non-believers don't recognise it as such.

The soul also offers extra powers of guidance but if they're not recognised, they simply lie dormant within us. So, those who **don't believe** in God, categorise the power that they carry within them as purely self-generated energy that's evolved over generations of human life, and later dies with the body.

But if that were the case, there would be no real purpose to life, which then makes it valueless.

So, let's compare the two options we have:
Example **a)** is a *Human Life Accepting God*
Example **b)** is a *Human Life Rejecting God*
Both have the same basic formula which is Flesh, Bone, Brain and your Soul.

The main difference comes in Decision Making, where in example **(a)** you don't only have Cerebral (Brain) power, but additionally, you have Soul Power. The soul delivers what is given by God. It can stimulate change, which the mind cannot do, and that's because the soul develops authority and purpose. However, in **b)** it lies dormant until you show a need for that authority.

By learning to use your intuition and instincts, you also awaken the creative side of your mind, and fire its imagination. By using a combination of your soul and your brain, you dynamise the choices you make, act more confidently, and achieve purposeful goals.

However, in **b)** this Soul Power lies dormant until you show a need for that authority.

But there are other differences too!
Again, if you subscribe to option **a)** you have additional powers activated within you
and one of these is Self Healing Power. There is a powerful healing that can be given at any time. You place your hands on your body where needed, and use prayer to ask God for healing to be given to rectify or ease any discomfort. This is helpful alongside medication.
In option **b)** this inner toll is available but remains dormant until it is called upon.

Prayer in option **a)** is an extremely powerful way of asking God for help and support. You can also pray to the Heavenly Host if you feel that you are wasting God's time on trivial things. You aren't, nothing is too trivial, but the other Hosts are there for you.

Prayer in option **b**) is not recognised and is not used.

Death after an Earthly Life in option **a**) your spirit returns home and continues its journey of growth and development in the Spirit Realms. That may include further lives on Earth or other planets. How exciting is that!

Death in option **b**) your spirit returns home and continues its journey of growth in the Spirit Realms, but it is less advanced.

The Constituents Of A Human Being:

- Your soul is there to help steer you to important points on your Life Map. They're the ones that provide those learning challenges for your development.
- Your brain is equipped with the basic abilities necessary to you on this journey. It's also influenced by the genes of your natural parents here on Earth. You may also carry a basis that relates to your life challenges, e.g. a life-threatening condition or disability.
- Your body is equipped for your journey in this life. It's also influenced by the genes of your natural parents. It may be fully able, or it may carry different levels of disability. Again, it's according to the needs chosen in your life challenges.
- You carry the benefits and problems experienced in one or more past lives. Negative energies may interfere with your life this time around and if that happens, they should be released by a regression therapist, otherwise they can block your development.

There are many formulae in life, and every choice, and move can be broken down into individual elements.

Of course, they can also carry a constant. Just as Pi is a constant in mathematics, life has its own.

So, let's look at two of the most valuable ones within your life.

Your Soul

The constant referred to as your 'soul' existed long before your life on Earth, and it'll continue its journey long after your human time here is over.

It's your core being and it's vital to your existence. It's also linked to another constant.

God

This amazing Creator Spirit Energy that many of us call God is ever present, whether that's recognised or not.

Our God not only serves Earth, but also serves some other inhabited planets within this Universe. But just as there are other Galaxies with planets within it, each living one has a God, and that's why I feel the word describes a Role, rather than just a Name.

So now you can see that there are two working constants within your life's formula, and they're linked.

For this life on Earth, you consist of a carefully balanced mix of both human 'material' (mind and body) and everlasting (soul/ spirit).

This construction helps you to weather the conditions here on Earth while you build on your experience and develop your power, wisdom and understanding from your chosen Earthly life. This must be done in a balanced way, and the co-planners of that life were you and God.

When you initially applied for a life on Earth you had reached a point of development, where certain areas of learning would benefit your growth, and these were best located within the Earth Plane. So, with guidance, you chose certain challenges appropriate to your level of learning within the Spirit Plane, and God took your application and constructed a proper working plan. He then put it into action at the necessary time.

This is the point where I must emphasise that **God is a part of life.**

No ifs, no buts.

God *is* part of the **Foundation of Life** and I'll explain more in Chapter 2

So, now we have your soul as one constant, and God as another. He is *crucial* to the creation and maintenance of life, and His Base is in the Spirit Realms.

The Soul In Detail

In August 2014, God talked to me about the soul, and explained its immense value to both our lives and to the planet itself, which then also makes it important to the Universe.

So often we view ourselves as isolated beings, but a lot more relies on us than we realise, and that applies to what we, as individuals bring to life as a whole.

Basically, the soul is a spirit that links you on Earth, or any other habitable planet, to an area within the Spirit Realms, where part of your soul still remains.

The part which powers your life here on Earth is within every cell of your body, and it's positioned perfectly to update the information relating to your every thought and action. Your brain may act in a separate way, but everything you do, and experience is also recorded within your soul's memory tank.

When a soul is initially formed by God it's given a quality that creates a power to develop, initially within the Spirit Realms, where it experiences quite rapid growth. That, in turn, is valuable to God's Think Tank which is also within the Realms.

The soul then follows a fascinating programme of growth within the area of learning that's deemed necessary, so that it will then develop necessary understanding.

Your Soul May Contribute To God's Think Tank

I think that the constant input of information shows how much God's Think Tank evolves through time. Whereas, in their perception of God, many religions seem to have stood still, as they continue to deliver a vision created long ago by mankind.

But, in truth, nothing stands still in this world or beyond, and God's Wisdom certainly isn't a stagnant force; it's infinite, and it's building within itself accurate knowledge gained from earlier development, plus the growing understanding that allows both a planet and its host Universe to develop.

Again, that opens up a picture of life beyond our own planet, and it gives us a need to look past 'our own backyard'.

I find it fascinating that God's Think Tank has various compartments of knowledge, and within each there are contributors, ensuring that the wealth of information continues to grow in a wide and beneficial way, to bring valuable growth.

In fact, God's values are an encircling act of growth brought on by mankind's contribution and those agents within spirit.

There's nectar within the Light that flows through God, and some of that value comes from people on Earth. This develops from understanding gained on the planet, and that's why there are Light and Dark energies within your soul.

When someone develops Light within their soul, it may also be a darker Light or a brighter one.

When a child is born it has the basis of Light within it, but it can't carry God's Light fully until it's around a year old.

At that point the child receives a boost of information, and the soul can then format in the way needed for his or her life.

If they're intelligent, they will obviously carry that extra benefit within the brain, but that may then override the need for growth within the soul until it's older. That's because they can already anticipate values through the mind, and at that point in life the value of the soul may seem inadequate to them.

Having said that, the brain is of little value compared with the soul, so I must emphasise that it's essential you develop more understanding of God's values and the purpose of your life here.

But because life on Earth has now been swayed by those with a more sterile teaching of logic through the brain, other values have been lost, and long term, mankind's *true* needs have become overlooked and meaningless. The knock-on effect of that is that it's depleted the soul's value, and lowered its vibrations, darkening the Light within it.

That's why we must restore true value and purpose through God and brighten that Light that shines out from within all our souls on Earth, because that will then bring good to the world, and few would argue that we do need that to happen.

The Versatility Of A Soul

As I said earlier, while part of your soul came to an Earthly life, another part still remains in your spirit home within the Realms.

There are many ways in which your soul can act when it's divided like this. It may simply be that a section of it continues to grow within your spirit home while the human part of you is living and developing on the Earth plane.

But there's also the possibility that it'll divide again to work and secure knowledge on a different realm, where there's a need to use its repatriation skills with souls who've acted criminally during their human life.

Although angels will already have repaired and healed those souls, there's a need for repatriation. It's an important step, because without it, there can still be a level of defiance and upset within a soul which doesn't allow it to act wisely. So, the solution is that the soul in question spends time with those who bring a level of authority and power, and that period of repatriation then enables them to move forward in an accountable way.

Those part souls who are in control, can fulfil their time by bringing authority to others, and at the same time, work towards their own growth. That is in the Spirit Realms. But away from there they *can't* live simultaneously with other parts of their soul on the *same* planet because it's not beneficial to their growth.

That's a power that's only given to those with a greater balance in their lives as a whole, and when permitted, it can bring great value and extra empowerment to them.

For the soul is a spirit within which many dimensions can come together over time, and form a powerful authority, whilst that soul's skills continue to grow.

So, let's talk briefly about the connection between the Earth Plane and that of the Spirit Realms.

In a simplistic way, it's rather like living in a downstairs apartment and having your greatest friends and relatives in another one upstairs. They're that close, and that's why communication is possible.

The Spirit Realms are home to our soul, as well as acting as base for God's incredible Spirit Energy making Him the *Host of All Energies.* So, as we're linked, we can all benefit from the ongoing drip, drip. drip of guidance and, when appropriate, empowerment.

God explained that although as humans, we're physically separate beings, through our souls we're connected to God's Power Source within the Spirit Realms, and ultimately, with all the other souls on Earth.

So, consider first that, like every baby in this world, you were born with an umbilical cord connecting you to your Earthly mother. Now visualise that your soul too has an unseen umbilical cord, that permanently connects you to God within the Spirit Realms, and that will show you how vital this connection is to your life on Earth and how closely we can all interact.

That link provides a valuable depth of backup support and knowledge throughout your time here, and that can enhance your ability and understanding to a far higher level, than if you had come to Earth with just a brain and a body, furthermore it's a knowledge that's topped up as necessary by the Source, God. In theory, how can you better that?

Well, the truth is that although you may believe that you're already making sufficient progress in the world, if you don't use your inner tools to keep a balance, you may be progressing in a less valuable direction, and the true purpose of your life here will still be hidden from you.

That's how simple it is to devalue your life by denying that connection with God and the spirit world in full. It's not just for the spiritual part of your life, because its practical guidance also sweetens your journey in other interesting ways.

Your Personal Growth

The level that your soul inhabits in the Realms depends on your overall point of development, and that in itself relies both on how successful your previous lives on Earth have been in achieving the goals you set yourself, and also on your level of learning in the Spirit Realms.

In fact, your Earthly existence is just a tiny part of your overall learning journey, however, it's particularly important because it's a time of free will that acts within a basis of good and evil.

We make choices on Earth, and within the Spirit Realms we are guided in the direction we need to pursue, so if we act positively our raw ambition can be helped by our experiences here during these lives on Earth. I say lives rather than life because it will take more than one to achieve what you need throughout your journey.

So How Do You Understand Life's Basic Need Of You

In some ways I wonder if life would be simpler if it came with an owner's manual. Just imagine, everything set out with clear explanations that told you why you're here, and what your purpose is within it all.

But then, not knowing the detail is part of the challenge. It's simply a bigger one if you're not in touch with all your senses.

If life is sailing along like a ship in calm waters you don't consider it the same, but when you encounter stormy conditions, you start to question, 'Why is this happening?'

It's then that you may refocus, and change direction. How much depends entirely on you and your chosen life challenges.

Please believe me when I say that changing focus, and being positive, really will open up your time here on Earth in a more powerful way, and when that happens you can achieve so much good, both for you and for the world.

Surely, the combination of climate change and the aftermath of the pandemic have forced a period of change on us all. It's leading us to reassess our lives, and two prominent questions are:

What's the purpose of my life here on Earth? Where does God come into it?

Currently the planet is dying because of both our actions and inactions. We step in when we shouldn't, and we stand back when we should be acting.

But so much is down to ignoring our soul messages and acting on outside influences with a different agenda. In order to heal the damage in the world, we must also focus on getting ourselves on course, because developing our futures in the right way, gives us the power and understanding to get the job done.

Focus On Your Journey

The first thing to do is make yourself more aware of the value of your life, and your needs. Once you've done that, you can put your heart and soul into your overall development. It's then that you'll begin to understand how valuable and tailored *you* are for your mission on Earth.

As humans we've been sold the need to focus on outward perfection. We may alter ourselves cosmetically in order to achieve a visual excellence, but that's only the short-term human packaging, and long-term soul value comes from within and is judged by God.

Interestingly God's most valuable blueprint for a human life, can intentionally carry flaws, because that then provides the opportunity for that person, and those close to them to discover new strengths and understanding. That in turn can act as a catalyst for positive changes in legislation, or development in health provision, sparking a powerful battle for change.

- So, if there's a question in your mind, asking why it's you who's suffering from cancer, motor neurone disease or some other debilitating condition, then realise now that your soul's brave choice of challenge is helping you to contribute to a greater understanding and cure. It can also help to raise people's awareness, and maybe eradicate the cause. It won't soften the blow of living with a disease, but the reason for it is there, and you can shift your focus to more constructive thoughts.

- Maybe you've looked at your child struggling to walk with leg callipers and questioned, 'Why him? Why her?'

   Again, we see the child rather than the soul within them that has made such brave choices for this life. So, we must support them and power them on, for their endurance and yours will go a long way towards making that journey a success. Maybe you'll raise precious funds or make the public more aware of the problems encountered through disability. So much needs to be changed, and these brave souls are playing an important role in the world.

- Did you feel that it was some sort of failure within *you* when you learned that your son or daughter was a Down's syndrome child or maybe autistic?

   It seems logical to accept blame when you feel your child is different and will face a more difficult life. But look at it from your soul's angle and God's, and that child is fulfilling a powerful journey of growth. Before their life on Earth, this soul requested a special quality of life that was more demanding, but also offered a higher opportunity of development.

   So, the choices were made, and God created the framework necessary to achieve that goal. The fact that the right parents and carers for that child are in place isn't an accident. They too came to this life in order to learn and offer support in this situation, as well as highlighting difficulties not yet recognised. For each person, life's path was laid so that lessons could be learned.

Sadly, the cultures of some countries, as well as certain religions have come up with their own answers to why these things happen, and frequently they can see these personal journeys as a failing or as God's judgement rather than the amazingly powerful lessons that they are. The result can be damning or at the very least, judgemental.

They show a bigotry that has no place in a tolerant world. But ignorance can bring out the worst in human thinking and there are still people who search for someone on which to hang the sign 'Sinner'.

Even now, negativity is often the default setting of a human mind, and the way in which God delivers our lessons can then be misunderstood.

Interestingly, on the 30th May 2022, my spirit guide,

Abuhindra spoke of …

The Need To Experience Hardship

He said that to make your future truly worthwhile, you need to be able to live with love and gratitude, and you cannot find fulfilment without it.

In his words, 'For a true way of living is in being a powerful person who holds within them an experience of hardship and understands that their stand in that situation allowed them to move forward entirely.'

He added, 'We all experience hardship, and it allows us to see and compare our life to others; and know that they too will experience it at some time, whether it's in the way you have or some other.'

He finished by saying, 'Divine Karma is a different way of hardship, for it is through that, that people pay for sins against humanity. They may feel they are equipped to cope but there will be that with which they cannot, and this is in direct payment for the harm they caused another.'

Speaking Personally, my own understanding has grown immensely over the years thanks to my work with God and His spirit representatives. I began with trust, and nervously acted on the spirit guidance given to me. Each time I learned, and at the same time, I gained confidence not just in God but in myself too, and that made me hungry to learn more.

Spirit's information has furnished me with some amazing facts, not only about life and its purpose, but also about what happens before this life on Earth, and also once it's over.

Even better, the knowledge that's been given to me provides an archive that I can share with you, so that *we all* understand life better, and fulfil our journey of learning.

So, let's move on to the subject of…

Balance

Some may argue that we have widened our knowledge through, what is seen as, a valuable scientific and technological approach, but at the same time we have ignored both the guidance and wisdom that lie within our own souls.

As a race, we have developed an 'out with the old, in with the new' vogue. We haven't repaired, adapted or made do, and we've applied the principle to life as a whole.

The soul and the brain are not there to be rivals, they are team players, and by not maintaining that status quo we create an imbalance, which isn't good for us or for the planet. There is an upside and a downside to consider.

For instance, the mobile phone is an immensely powerful tool that helps us in so many ways, but how many people no longer communicate with those around them when they're at a coffee bar, restaurant or even at home, because they're on their phone?

In the same way, the focus on brain power has eclipsed the need for soul wisdom, and yet that balance is vital to our future.

Balance is something that God has shown me to be of vital importance to life. In fact, within the sentences of several prayers that He has given me over the years, the word 'balance' is prominent, as is the negativity of 'imbalance'.

Here are extracts from some of my current prayers:
1. 'I ask now for healing to be given to correct imbalance.'
2. 'Let me be wiser for it to balance my life better…'
3. 'Let it be that I am given a way forward of true power, by devising a way of true balance; so that I may achieve my goals in full…'
4. 'Let no rejections be given for the way forward to be of true balance again.'
5. '…and that will bring both the need to serve God, but also the need to serve the Earth in its imbalance.'
6. 'And let it be that they bring a quality and equality to the world, and not an imbalance that shakes the world of its vitality and allows a worsening of its health too.'

The last example paints an especially clear picture.

Referring back to my time as a motor mechanic, an engine that's out of balance can't produce the power that a balanced one can. In the same way, the units that deliver that power to the wheels must also have the best possible balance because otherwise that power cannot be delivered efficiently, and valuable energy is lost.

It's just the same in our lives, and I'm not just talking about mind power versus soul power, I'm including the practical areas of our lives like balancing our work and rest as well as the type of foods we eat because that's **our** fuel.

So, returning to the subject of life guidance, in this technological era, the focus has moved from the quieter instinctive messaging that comes from our soul, and the shouty logic that now governs a large part of decision making throughout the world.

Both as a whole, and individually we're seriously out of balance; focusing solely on what logic tells us we want out of life, but not including what life needs from us.

There's so much more to our journey here on Earth than a brain led route can ever provide, and as long as the emphasis remains on its development, our time here will lack the true achievement and richness we seek.

The result is instability, negativity, and a dying planet. And that's because not only are we not fully appreciating the Role of God, but we're also using a fraction of the inner tools we possess. The route of humankind is expected to satisfy every need, but it can't achieve that, because it can't fully nourish the human mind, body, *and* soul.

Earning money and struggling to achieve a material status in a world obsessed by wealth, still leaves a lot of people hungry, both in the practical sense, and in a spiritual way. It also knocks the whole world off balance, including the planet itself.

And the time has now come where we must return it to a point of equilibrium, where humanity achieves its true purpose, and life can once again nourish us all and help us to feel rewarded. But that *is not possible* without the Power of God.

Speaking Personally, over recent years I have come to understand the true meaning and purpose of life, and how our own power and weaknesses affect far beyond our planet.

We can all achieve more if we learn the basis of life, and the Role of God. Some of the information that I deliver may be outside your current understanding, but give it space to settle, and if later on you want more detail, there will be specialist areas that you can research.

One surprise along my own spiritual journey, was that guidance given by spirit can often be practical.

For example, early on in my relationship with my guides, I was told that I needed to help in the world. My immediate reaction was of desperation, 'Where do I start?' So, I asked that very question, and was told to begin by sponsoring a child in a poor country, and with the help of my husband, Mike, and a small spiritual group I'd drawn together, we began sponsoring Ahmed in Ethiopia. That later developed into setting up with my friends, a charity that sponsored eleven children, helped homeless people in the UK and later took aid to Eastern Europe. I can't tell you how rewarding that was inwardly, and what wonderful people I met as a result. But even more, it also taught me how much more I was capable of doing.

For me, there are huge benefits from working with the guidance and empowerment given by God, whether it's direct channelling as I do or simply using our instinctive and intuitional guidance. Each day, I use the valuable help, but **this guiding power is here for us all**, so don't doubt its presence or God's.

When You Accept or Reject God

On the 28th October 2022, I received this message from Abuhindra, which is so pertinent to our future:

'For a way forward blessed with authority, we must ensure that people understand and believe that God exists. For there are no ways of replicating that Power, and the issue is of great importance to all who live in the world today. So, this must be emphasised because then the authority will exist that can repair the whole planetary upset.'

I must say again that although we're all free to make our choice about God, if you choose to exclude that vital constant, from your life equation, your inner satnav will remain unused, life's hurdles will appear higher, your true power will be less, and you may end up lost within a maze of human logic.

Which makes life on Earth problematic and far less rewarding, and surely, we have never needed help and guidance more than we do now in this troubled world.

For the non-believer, whether or not they accept it as fact, they'll still end up in the Spirit Realms after this life is over, because all souls make the journey home.

They won't have developed as much as those who accept God, their overall understanding will be less, and their next life on the Earth plane will already be booked, in the hope that next time they'll achieve all the things they failed to succeed at this time around.

The Variables In Life's Formula

The object of a life here on Earth is to gain an authority that comes from a package of learning and experience, and for some, that will include tests of endurance and varying levels of suffering.

Life's purpose can be achieved in many ways, and our individual challenges and journeys provide an opportunity to develop a greater understanding through experience. That can then open up opportunities for each of us on our return to the Spirit Realms.

When someone develops the understanding that comes with suffering, it provides an empowering type of learning, and their life may change as a result. On Earth, they have the free will to choose whether that power and knowledge will enable them to develop and fulfil a vital and positive route in life, or whether they will allow the experience to make them negative.

It's one thing to decide the area of learning that you need to develop when you're still a soul resident in the Spirit Realms, but once you're living that planned life on Earth, it may seem very different. You may not remember your choices, and if the strong influences around you succeed in persuading you to see the situation in a negative way, you will have to be very determined if you are to develop a powerful route forward.

But first, let's imagine that these examples are what you (in spirit form) submitted to God as a basic *'journey plan'* for a future life on Earth. In simple terms:
1. ***You chose to experience and overcome the pain of losing a loved one....*** like a child, a parent, a sibling, or a partner.

Within the framework that He creates for this life, God will draw together:
- The soul that needs to experience the loss of their own life.
- Those who need to go through the agony of losing a loved one.
- The opportunity to learn and bring some good from the experience.

This is the blueprint and it's carefully programmed. After all, God is the Ultimate Programmer.

Later, on Earth, those involved, who have a belief in God, can pray for help and support for this difficult time. The result is that they'll be given the strength to deal with this painful situation.

So, how do you draw something positive from such a negative situation?

Maybe it's by raising funds for those with the same condition/ illness, or by joining others who are attempting to improve the healthcare system. It may mean helping others who are suffering in the same way, or, if appropriate, petitioning for a change in legislation.

Whatever you can do to bring something positive from that painful experience helps you to cope and ensures that when that person died something positive grew from the memory.

2. ***You chose to be an influencer in the world.***

There are so many ways you can achieve this, but if you're aware of your inner guidance, a direction will be apparent to you. It may be on a local scale where you recognise, and play a part in ironing out inequalities, or maybe your love of animals will take you in a different direction. Of course, as we all face the various difficulties of climate change, your work may also direct you to worrying areas of planetary upset.

Do not confuse being an influencer for human values, with the so called 'influencers'who are the scourge of the internet, who are looking for something for nothing for a mention on their social medial pages.

Whatever you focus on, God and His spirit helpers will be there to empower you.

Each Day Has Its Challenges

Without doubt, there are lessons waiting for you every day of your life. Discounting your spiritual purpose, you still face a daily barrage of practical and mental challenges. They're a mix of the simple, and more complex issues that you must deal with personally, or within your workday, and they all contribute to that big picture which you call 'My life'.

But if you focus in a positive way, you'll develop a balance that feeds you spiritually, mentally, and physically; and you'll be better prepared for the difficulties that arise, which you can then learn to manoeuvre around. When life becomes simpler it becomes much friendlier and you can build on your adventure.

The way that you deal with these challenges also helps to mould you into the person you ultimately become. So, the better the balance, the more that you'll benefit.

If you're someone who handles each part of the day in a positive way, it will be easier to overcome the ups and downs than if you're negative. You'll also see opportunities where negativity can blind you to them. It's all part of a balanced journey and on a worldwide scale, it's vital to the future of humanity.

The Power Of Symmetry

With so much focus on brain development, the richness of our other natural skills can remain unused, and if we're not careful they will be completely smothered by a blanket of logic. So, in order to avoid that, we must adjust the scales and reawaken some of those God given gifts.

Your soul is a treasure chest of important memories and understanding, so when it's given the opportunity, it can act as your inner satnav.

But early on, if you are to achieve your goals, you must invest the effort necessary to discover your true guidance. Later, you'll naturally tune in, but first you must learn to calm your brain's noisier logic, so that it doesn't drown out your soul's more subtle messages.

This is wisdom that doesn't explain the reason for its guidance, but that again trains you to trust more. So allow your gut feeling to reassure you. The reasons will become apparent to you later.

Just as your heart guides you to subjects that fire your passion, your conscience ensures that you take a moral route, and your soul guides you instinctively. These are all vital tools that you possess.

But no matter how well equipped you are, it's possible that even when these instincts stir you into action, you may end up ignoring them. Why?

Well, I'm sure that like me, there have been times where you've sat and considered some things so long that eventually other thoughts came in and 'talked you out' of what you were planning. So, you about turned and rejected everything that you were initially so focused on doing.

That's called, 'Having second thoughts' and we all do on occasions.

But these thoughts come from your brain, and suddenly your logic is taking over. So be firm, be brave and don't let it derail you. You'll find the exercise on being guided by your soul in Section 2

Of course, the main purpose of your life, and that meaningful journey, can begin at any point. The conditions and timing depend on what area of growth your soul has chosen to follow. But that doesn't diminish the importance of your senses at any point in your life because the practicalities of each day, your diet, your level of fitness, relaxation and general guidance will be encompassed in the information that your inner satnav/soul feeds you. So don't think that the time's not right yet. It is.

You'll feel sharper and more focused for your life in general which, of course, puts you a step ahead of others. Suddenly, it'll be you they turn to for inspiration.

Have you ever wondered how the most successful sportsmen like F1 drivers, rally drivers, tennis players, jockeys and others achieve that extra magic that places them at the top of their careers?

It's not just training, although that's essential. They also learn to work with their senses so they can perfectly judge the line and speed into a corner, the angle and strength of strike to win a point on a tennis court, or the moment to urge forward a horse to win. It's a careful balance of logic and awareness. Even successful scientists and the wizards of technology must have initially used their senses to direct their own powerful areas of research.

How else would they have found the inspiration to begin? They stepped into the unknown without proof of their abilities. They knew it was right. But then most narrowed their choices and focused on the limitations of brain power.

Just as your areas of spirit development can vary a great deal from those of others, they can also be time sensitive, and when you continue to ignore directional guidance that will lead you to your spiritual challenges, you may run out of time to complete them. If that happens, you have to come back to another life in order to finish that section of learning. But for that to happen you have to ignore a lot of obvious guidance.

However, because you earlier committed to these choices, any unfinished journey is not scrapped and replaced with something new for your next life on Earth. The earlier challenge is still crucial to your development, and so it must be completed.

But when you focus your attention on your soul's messages of guidance, it can help you to achieve the balance that will serve your life as a whole. Your senses will be sharper and more alert to the signals that take you forward, and that will give you a good start, no matter what age you are.

God's Energy and Empowerment can also be there for every part of your life, whether it's practical or spiritual. After all, God understands that you succeed more when your life is well balanced, and unnecessary stress is lifted, so never doubt that it's the soundest route to take.

The brain does have a creative side as well as a logical one, but in this scientific and technological era so many of us are overwhelmed by the need for logic, that it often doesn't allow our individuality to grow, and that in turn, makes it harder for us to achieve the goals we chose so long ago. So instead, we move like sheep along the same narrow path as everyone else, and a sameness develops instead of that wonderful individuality we came to express.

Speaking Personally, it reminds me of a quirky song called 'Little Boxes' that was sung in the 1960s by the folk singer, Pete Seeger.

Little boxes on the hillside
Little boxes made of ticky-tacky
Little boxes on the hillside
Little boxes all the same
There's a green one and a pink one
And a blue one and a yellow one

And they're all made out of ticky-tacky
And they all look just the same
And the people in the houses
All went to the university
Where they were put in boxes
And they came out all the same
And there's doctors and lawyers
And business executives
And they're all made out of ticky-tacky
And they all look just the same
Source:
Songwriters: Malvina Reynolds
LyricFind

Well, you get the idea!

Find Your Own Way

Follow your gut feeling, and don't miss those instinctive messages.

It can be difficult stepping outside your comfort zone but remember that it's strengthening you as a whole.

Of course, opposition comes in different ways:
- Your *culture* may try to influence you to change paths, but if inwardly you feel that your soul is guiding you along a correct and moral direction, do you need to change?
- Your *parents'* wishes for your life may be different to yours. Again, you must weigh up the options.
- Your *schoolteachers,* or your *employers* may want to mould you for careers that don't excite you. If inwardly you have a passion to fulfil, and this feels the right time, then stay strong and focused.

I feel that many religions promise their followers a reward in Heaven but they explain little about the personal relationship that they can have with God here on Earth.

Centuries of mankind's influence have tailored a vision of God that suits the needs of each religion, and yet that vision seems divorced from life in the 21st century.

So, when the subject of God is presented in a way that's unconvincing, people focus on more tangible influences, and easier goals. Financial and material benefits present a fresh manmade dogma, and the focus moves from helping others to self-promotion, so spiritual growth slips down the list of priorities.

There's a difference between wanting something and needing it. I have found it a useful benchmark in my life, just as my conscience is my guide.

It doesn't mean that you have to do without, but when the *Inner You* tells you, *The Person,* 'I really need to do this' and you act on it, you'll find that your level of fulfilment will increase, and you'll respect yourself more.

Focusing solely on human goals of self-achievement may bring you short term satisfaction, but overall, your life will become less rewarding.

Whereas, when you follow your soul's instinctive direction, you'll develop a better balance because God's Power and Guidance will help you achieve a better quality of life. Once you commit to that, you realise your days are flowing better.

Many people believe they know what's best for you, but only you and God truly know, and that guidance is there within your soul. Act on it, and it'll focus you on the direction you need to take. You'll develop a powerful passion for life.

Of course, our true core can stay buried for a long while.

Speaking Personally, I didn't become completely true to myself until later in life. Before that, I followed my parent's choices. I was taught that they were older and wiser.

I had a fulfilling life as a wife and mother, but before that area of spiritual freedom opened up to me, my views and needs were governed by a strict upbringing, and family loyalty.

So, in my new passion as a spiritual healer and all that followed, I discovered a part of me that I hadn't appreciated before, and my life has since become more valuable. As a bonus, my husband, Mike has been happy to follow his own valuable path of discovery as we've developed our spiritual journeys together.

I had no idea where my purposeful path would take me, but it captivated me, and taught me to free myself of the limitations of logic and instead feed my ambition. Inspirational thoughts set my imagination on fire, and that led me along routes that I never thought I would travel. I'm still on that adventure and I thank God every day for it, and the good it's brought.

Sometimes You Must Compromise

If you can only partly commit to your own spiritual development, do it and gradually allow other elements of your journey to fall into place. Work with it and you'll find the freedom to fulfil your true purpose here on Earth. So don't see your situation as unworkable because God will help you to blend this new direction into your existing life, with your spiritual development running alongside other commitments.

As your passion grows, your choices will reflect change, and your core needs will be fulfilled.

Just quieten that logic and trust the wisdom within your soul.

Whatever age you are, start taking steps to ***find your purpose, and act on your soul's guidance.***

Of course, a life of development can bring both good and bad experiences but mix in the human element and it can become more complicated, because humankind has its own agenda, which may not follow God's needs or our original development blueprint. So, to come through these situations in a powerful way, we must revert to God's Wisdom and Guidance.

The pandemic is over, but the pain remains for many. It may have begun as a serious health issue from which many have died, but the knock-on effect has also badly damaged many people's livelihoods and security. Those who avoided Covid, may have escaped health worries, but instead found that any pre pandemic normality, has been wiped away and a programme of hardship has taken its place. This has been further complicated by another war within the world.

Every day our scale of endurance, determination and love is tested. Never before has it been so essential that we use all our inner skills to survive and help others to do so as well. After all, this is a time where past helpers may need assistance, and those who've been helped in the past need to bring aid to others.

So, focus on your soul's instinctive messages, learn to be intuitive, follow those gut feelings, and become a more complete version of you.

Just Remember

Your heart and soul may at times tug at your conscience and tell you that you should do certain things. But the soul has a softer voice than your brain's logic, so it's mainly in the quiet contemplative times that you'll become aware of it.

So, how do you take control of your life choices?

In your teens: Your spiritual awareness may have been dulled by the influence of logic from parents, teachers, friends, persuasive advertising etc, and your brain may still rule alone.

But if any of those influencers do recognise the need for a balance between soul and brain power, they'll encourage you to act on inspiration, and thoughts, that can help you to establish some early spiritual skills. Even where there is a disability, your quality of life can improve when you act on your soul's wisdom.

At each stage of your life, you need to remember that you are mind, body, and spirit/ soul, and just as you invest in caring and cultivating your mind and soul, you should apply the same care to your body because it's part of your life equation. I'll enlarge on this in Section 2.

Later, your mind and body may need more focus as intolerances develop. Physically weaknesses may become evident, and your mind may carry the strains brought on by life, but that doesn't mean your lessons end there. Instead, that's when life guides you to some new goals.

The more senior you become, the more you must learn to flex your mental and spiritual muscles, in order to cope with both eventualities and opportunities that age imposes. But alongside attending to your own needs, this is also a time for bringing inspiration to others and helping **them** discover their own awareness and opportunities.

Your life choices are your own so, do you wrap yourself up in a coat of self-indulgence and see only the bad in life, or look outside your own needs and face the day with interest and determination?

Where life previously served up a cocktail of action, the older version of you may focus more spiritually where you inspire others with your positive outlook.

Accepting help may make you humble, but that's just another vital aspect of a powerful new lesson.

Humility

First let's separate the positive force of 'Humility' from the negativity of 'Humiliation'.

I was fascinated to learn from Abuhindra, that even in the Spirit Realms, humility is vital to your progress, no matter what level you're at.

Some in power on Earth have developed a degree of untouchability and arrogance but that's control rather than power and it's not God given. Instead, it's a cheap imitation of the real thing. But a few can surprise you with their true sincerity.

For humility and true power go together in life, and whether it's here on Earth or home in the Spirit Realms, by being truly humble, it lays the foundation for a powerful future.

Let's examine that more.

We see God as the most powerful Spirit Energy linked with Earth, but as part of that life formula, God *serves* our needs within the world, guiding and empowering us to fulfil our goals. Likewise, we are supposed to *serve* God by serving the world where needed. That means within the human race, the animal kingdom, and the planet itself. By doing that it boosts our development, and together with a raised understanding and our love, that makes us more powerful.

So never look down on those who serve, instead play your part too.

I've found along my own spiritual development that some of my happiest and most rewarding times have been spent serving others in their need, and it powers me on to do more.

So, to sum up, don't be afraid of where soul guidance will take you. Be aware of your gut feeling and follow the direction that feels right. Allow the positivity to flow through you. When you make that commitment, you'll find that God is there to help you fulfil it. You'll feel empowered, which will enable you to focus better. It'll help develop and guide you to plan with the precision that allows you to achieve more.

But what if the pressures are on you to follow a different route? For instance:

Problem 1: Because you love, respect and may want to please your parents, and other family members, you

may have felt duty bound to adopt some of their opinions and tendencies, which simply don't sit right with you.
Answer: This is your life, not theirs. Ultimately, they should respect your need to follow your own conscience, beliefs, and understandings of what is right.

Problem 2: Certain teachers and influencers may have guided you in ways that no longer apply to your life.
Answer: Then take the advice that sits well with you and build your future in the positive way you feel is right.

Problem 3: Maybe you took up a career that wasn't your choice, because you wanted to be loyal or please someone other than yourself.
Answer: Be comfortable in your role to give of your best. Why work in a mediocre way when you can do what you really ***need*** with passion? If that's not possible, can you combine elements of spiritual development alongside?

Problem 4: You may hold certain values because of peer pressure.
Answer: If deep down you don't believe others' values are right for you, stop chasing them!

Problem 5: Society or some authority may have influenced you in a way that doesn't make you feel good about yourself. It doesn't sit well with your conscience.
Answer: Break out and show your true colours. You may end up a leader rather than a follower.

Problem 6: Advertisers are persuasive, but do you really need it or desire it?
Answer: Don't abandon your instincts. Instead show you don't agree and become an influencer.

Problem 7: Do you follow a monetary route because you think it's the only way, but you still feel empty?

Answer: Money is a necessary tool in our human life but it's not a god. Develop an alternative route, that fulfils you. But also be aware that money may sometimes open doors to opportunity so don't ignore the chance for positive development.

Problem 8: Do you struggle to keep up with the highflyers? Do you question the mental and physical stress you're experiencing through it?

Answer: Weigh up the pros and cons. Is your health suffering? Are your relationships affected by such pressures? What is life worth to you? It's time to be honest, and act on what you decide.

Remember that at any point, your life may have become cluttered by directions, and outlooks, that don't fit your personal life mould. They may gradually erode your determination, so assess what's of value in your life, and discard those things that aren't.

It's like wearing someone else's shoes. They need to fit if they are to be comfortable. Anything else is unwanted.

Some people may not be happy when you make that move, and they may try to dissuade you. You may even find that you need to move away from certain social circles that no longer fulfil you, but others will replace them as you become the person you need to be.

You *are* important! You *are* unique so celebrate it, and don't hide it!

Act out *your* own role in life, rather than other people's. Be honest with yourself and your life will flow better, it'll make you feel good, and you'll achieve more.

Being the best that you can be doesn't require you to be a celebrity, or a millionaire, or even an award-winning musician, but if you are, you'll be among the best.

Even if you're never publicly recognised, God will know who you are, and *you* will know you've given the best you can.

So, consider what you're doing, and whether it benefits your life. Have you been acting out of habit and not even noticed? Become aware of yourself and change what needs changing!

Speaking Personally, I can honestly say that for me, although it took me a long while to discover my own spiritual journey, my life has been so much more of an adventure, as over the past 26 years I have committed to work and development that I would never have imagined doing, like starting and running our charity, delivering furniture and aid boxes to UK homeless and driving vehicles filled with a wide range of aid out to Eastern Europe, as well as helping offenders who were in prison or on probation. These were all such unknown areas to me, but I grew my understanding and the fulfilment I have gained from it all has been immense.

Interestingly, it was my spirit guide, Jesus who guided me to take aid to Serbia as well as Croatian schools, homeless centres, and children's homes after the Balkans War.

I met with doubt and reluctance in the UK as I tried to locate contacts in Serbia, but a newscaster put me in touch with the Red Cross and United Nations in Geneva, and they directed me to the Crveni krst in Sremski Karlovci. We became the first British people officially in 8 years to have entered the country and were met with warmth and friendship.

We each have the ability to develop our lives according to that original blueprint, and the more we focus on that, the greater value our own lives will be, and our world and even the Universe will benefit.

Chapter Two: Understanding God

Including: What Is Belief; Why God? Power Within The Universe; God's Place Within Our Human Existence; God And Religion; Living Without God; So, What's In A Word; Learning The Truth About God; So Why Is The Planet Suffering; God, War And Terrorism; Personally Speaking; The Foundation Of Life The Energies That Surround Us; God's Wisdom; Programmer Extraordinaire; God's Role Within The Universe; More Detail On God's Role.

First, let's ask

What Is Belief?

According to the Cambridge dictionary, the meaning of BELIEF is a state or habit of mind in which trust, or confidence is placed in some person or thing.

That can be applied to both God and Science. But when it comes to facts about spirit, science hasn't yet found a way to either prove or disprove its presence, and we therefore have a level playing field.

So, please exercise this trust because there's nothing to lose and a lot to gain by accepting God, but if you don't, you may fail to awaken that understanding that exists deep within you, and that will impede your journey in life.

So, let's now ask:

Why God?

Earlier, I asked that you accept my word that God is an essential part of each day, and your life as a whole. Now I must explain why.

I imagine that like mine, your basic knowledge of God has probably been that taught by one of many

religions. They each deliver their own slant on this Deity, and so it may seem to you that God is:
1. Only accessible if you follow a religious path.
2. Unbelievable because there's no proof of God's existence, and religion doesn't convince you.
3. Solely the Deity for this world.
4. An uncaring God who does nothing for us.

So, confusion continues to grow and help to fuel science's conclusion that there is no such Spirit Being as God.

Yet, the truth is that God is an integral part of the Foundation of Life, not only here on Earth, but also on some other planets within this Galaxy.

It was interesting to me when recently a Healer friend said that most of the scientific people she had worked with during her time at university, didn't believe in God.

The problem is that when we reject an important part of the picture, we limit our overall understanding, and therefore important detail can be lost to us. So, let's fill in a bit more of what that involves.

Power Within the Universe

We're all familiar with the concept of hierarchies within our own world, and although we may not always agree with them, they exist and they are human beings who fulfil the roles of decision makers, the architects for life in the future, and of course control managers.

Interestingly, levels of power also exist beyond our own planet, and my powerful spirit correspondents have told me that there are many immense Spirit Energies placed throughout the Universe, who act as overseers.

The Role of God exists many times over. In fact, within every Galaxy there's a God that brings new creation to each planet once it shows a need for life. But before that can happen, decisions must be made by those overseeing the Universe's overall development. They then use their authority to invite God to fulfil His Role of Creator and Protector and allow new life to begin.

These powerful beings are united in their need to sanction new life opportunities which can then promote growth, and they are part of a hierarchy throughout the Universe that works to allow goodness to spread and greater understanding to be achieved.

Such wisdom is good for everyone, and it enables each within the hierarchy to report and transfer knowledge from one Galaxy to another. If it resonates well with them, they too adopt the processes that can then bring growth, and that in turn, will result in a more vibrant and powerful Universe as a whole.

When that vibrancy reaches a power that's acceptable to those beings who oversee the entire Universe, then they in turn are able to bring vision and the concept of a new and animated life throughout. And that can benefit each one within our collection of Universes.

So, just as I talked earlier of the far-reaching effect of our own power and balance, we can see here how it can affect the overall wellbeing both within our planet and beyond it.

So, let's move on to the subject of God, and whether this Deity is simply an optional part of life as a whole.

God Within Our Human Existence

In actual fact, God is the Supreme Being that brings growth and power to both our world and beyond, and it's God's Presence that ensures that there's not a stagnant power governing the planet.

Yet, there are still many people here on Earth who believe that the human race develops itself, and there's no God. The answer is that it's *not* possible, because **we are unable to grow without the life force that God brings**, so we *cannot develop* without it.

God And Religion

When we look at the relationship between God and religion, there's much confusion, but no matter how well-meaning or well-presented a particular religion is, God *is* separate to religion!

Equally, religion is not God, although some may purport to bring the Worth of God to the world.

Inevitably, the formulae are different.

Where Religion's Version of God is:

Religion's God = Human Interpretation of God + Language Differences + Cultural, Political, and Personal Biases

God's Direct Version is simpler:

God = God

To define religion as a whole wouldn't be fair. At their best, each Faith can draw people to a belief in God and principles welcomed by God. At their worst they can be used more for the benefit of those in authority, rather than for their congregation.

Religion's version of God is inevitably presented with a human essence. Senior religious authorities can bring their vision, politics, culture, and bias to the fore, which may play an active part in their representation of God.

Pagans believe that Earth is the authoritative power, but although the planet has a valuable energy, it's not the Ultimate Creative Energy. It's simply **an important part of the whole**, and when those who worship the Earth don't recognise God, they're only accepting **part** of the truth.

It's interesting to see that although many people shy away from religion, figures of Buddha abound in many homes and gardens, and not just those of Buddhists. Their visual promise of serenity has won the hearts of many who seek a symbol of peace.

Living Without God

So, why is it that many now walk away from the concept of God, by whatever Name used?

It seems there's a lack of understanding as to who or what God is, and there have also been people of influence who over centuries have brought a level of fear and untouchability about God, because it gained them an authority over others. But you can't preach in one sentence that God is Love, and then bring a list of conditions before that Love can be given. Add to that, the negativity within which we now live, and it pushes the positive concept of God out of reach.

In this more liberated 21st century there is an underlying fear and apprehension. We call it *Stress*. It applies to many areas of life where we compete to fulfil human expectations. Early on it can even cost young lives.

Later there's the practical stress of not having a job, then when you achieve that, there's the stress of meeting targets, not being able to pay the mortgage, not being able to fulfil the expectations of your family, children, parents etc., and overall, there's the fear of failing!

The news you read is mainly negative, it focuses on failures and is often sensationalising. So, then your expectations of life become lower, and if that weakens your mental and physical health it adds to the problems.

Without God there can be an aloneness.

So, What's in a Word?

As someone who works with God, I have researched versions of religious words that have been used to project Him, as well as some that God uses in His channelled information.

The harshness shown in some religious words has never sat right with my positive vision of God as an ever-present Spirit Friend and Guide. For me, there are two different portrayals here and they are both listed in the dictionary.

1. **Mercy**

Negative Meaning: Someone begging for *Mercy* from a harsh God.

Positive Alternative: This is the *Compassion* that God offers.

Two clear dictionary variations on the same word. I choose the second.

2. **Fear** ('Fear God in Life' is the Motto of the Somerville Clan)

Negative Meaning: *Fear* is being used as a tool for control.

Positive Alternative: *Respect*.

I believe respect is important to life as a whole, and certainly to God.

3. **Dread** ('Dread God' is the Motto shared by Clan Munro and Clan Carnegie.)

Negative Meaning: Living in *Dread* and particularly of God's Judgement.

Positive Alternatives: *Revere* and *Deeply Respect*.

For me there's no contest. Revering God is natural to me. Yes, I deeply respect Him.

4. **Worship**

The word *'Worship'* may not have a negative application, but it has in the past been interpreted by some as requiring human or animal sacrifices which I see as negative.

A more positive meaning of the word that sits well with me in my understanding of the Creator is the meaning, 'To show **respect**, to love, to show *reverence'*.

In fact, I have learned that worship doesn't just apply to God. It includes loving and respecting yourself and others, as well as each day of your life, the world around you, and so much more. The theme here is clearly Respect.

5. **Devout**

The word *Devout* is a bit old fashioned and many would simply apply its meaning to a religious follower of God.

But when you replace it with the dictionary's alternatives, *'devoted'* and *'sincere'*, I think they're probably more user friendly in today's world.

6. **Worth**

Unsurprisingly, the dictionary's first interpretation of Worth is financial, but doesn't that reflect our change in values?

Look further down the list and another version offers the more personal explanation, 'The level at which someone or something deserves to be valued or rated '.

Learning The Truth About God.

So many words can be manipulated, whether they're used to sell you a car, or persuade you to view God in a particular way. But we need clarity, especially now, and as you can see by the words above, we can switch easily from a negative viewpoint to a positive one if we choose, and that can help our day to flow better.

Sadly, in human terms, the subject of God has been translated, assessed, and passed through many political and cultural filters over the centuries, developing wide ranging views of what God is and needs of us. But the sanitized versions have led to many people walking away not just from religion's God, but also from the real One, because they haven't trusted the versions offered to them.

Once that trust is lost, even if others speak of the true and rich relationship that you can have in a one to one with God, they may be wasted words.

But those who deliver a true vision of God, and I include myself here, can only ever be the messengers; so, the more you learn to trust and develop your own communication with God, especially for His guidance, the stronger your life will become. Just, never doubt that He is with you.

Developing your own relationship with God, you learn direct how to assess and develop your life, and then you can recognise where outside influences do or don't feel right.

It avoids the editing and distortion that can come when you rely on others to interpret for you.
- After all, they may misinterpret the original message and unwittingly change the meaning.
- When a message reaches others, consciously or unconsciously they may put their own interpretation on it, so truth can get watered down or changed. I think that history has shown many examples of that.

But when there are two meanings in a sentence, it's down to the individual how they interpret that. I'll show you an example which comes within the daily prayers given to me by God. This particular one can be interpreted two ways:

'I am the capacity to do God's work, and I shall bring forward a knowledge of that power and wisdom that God gives to all people.'

Now does that mean that I will bring forward that knowledge to all people, or does it mean that God already gives that knowledge to all people, and I will confirm it within my work?

In this instance it doesn't really matter because in both ways, people receive the information, but in some other situations it may matter a lot, and it illustrates how important it is that we get a clear picture of God, and what He is telling us.

The meanings of words can be used to sway people's thinking and belief, and in a world ruled by politics and other leaders, too often words *are* used as a manipulative tool.

Sadly, the portrayal of God has for many years stood still, while life on Earth has moved on in so many ways. But in truth just as we evolve, so does God's understanding of our needs.

This Divine Spirit told me long ago that He is the Host of All Energies, and that means that He is aware of all changes however large or small. The communication between the Earth plane and the Spirit plane constantly updates God's Thinktank, so this incredibly Powerful Spirit Energy is fully aware of your needs and will see them even before you do.

So Why is the Planet Suffering?

Why are we now enduring such troubled lives?

Our world delivers a basis of equal and opposing values of good and evil and together with that we each have free will.

This was the result of careful planning by the Universe's overseeing powers with a need to bring forward a different experience and understanding, and the blueprint given to God was to create life according to those parameters.

Of course, that offers the human race a great freedom of choice. We can choose between good and evil, and equally, we can do that without reference to God, so mistakes and bad judgements are inevitable; even when we do wrong it can bring a more powerful lesson than if we were restricted to a more positive route.

But humankind has taken that further, because step by step, human intelligence has developed, and because the brain is a ***visible*** harbour of wisdom and the soul ***is not***, it has become the full focus for development.

But there is an old German proverb, 'Don't throw out the baby with the bath water', and that is just what we've done, because the brain has been developed at the cost of the soul. And not only is that constant the very essence of us, but it's also our link to that other vital one, God.

So gradually, human understanding has been downgraded to a level where it no longer realises its true power or value, and that affects both us as individuals and the planet as a whole.

When we rely on a limiting brain led intelligence, we distance ourselves from the reality of God, and an afterlife, because the brain lacks the understanding of the soul. That then affects our inner balance, because the brain was designed to be one part of the intelligence base for our human life, and on its own it can't fulfil those vital life goals, especially as the second part of that force is constantly updated and empowered to fulfil life's journey. So, without the soul's power and connection, we're heading downstream without a paddle.

For those who ignore it, the soul will continue to deliver a basic life energy until it's given time is over and it returns to the Spirit Realms, but without our interaction that's all it provides. Meanwhile, its guidance and empowerment tools will remain untapped.

God, War and Terrorism

By devising our own 'development route' and rejecting God's, the human race has developed a tendency to enhance the negative forces in life.

We came to this life to focus on the development that we chose, and to enrich life on Earth along the way. The direction is of positive learning, caring, and understanding. Yet now the focus is on a different sort of wealth. It's a more selfish route that says, 'This is mine, and not yours.' That leads to dissatisfaction, war, and control.

We've been on this planet long enough now that we have had plenty of opportunities to increase our understanding, and develop tolerance, but too many members of the human race can still find an excuse for a fight. So, although religious and cultural wars should be a thing of the past, the world is still very divided, and one of God's Names is frequently used to express control whether it's led by race or gender dominance.

- There is nothing in God's Creed that promotes the value of a man over that of a woman. Such differences destroy equality, and they originate with mankind.
- There is nothing in God's Creed that promotes one religion to go to war against another, if each is true to God, no matter what respectful Name they use.
- Race and colour differences become the excuse for violence and yet none are sanctioned by God.
- Terrorists shout their loyalty to God through their religious beliefs. They commit horrific crimes, both killing and maiming those who belong to another religion or are non-believers.

But the common denominator that everyone sees is religion, and to many that means that God is the catalyst. So, there's no wonder many people decry both.

Yet if we look honestly, it's humankind's evil acts that we're seeing, and in no way a true representation of God, who abhors such cruelty. Those who hold a need for control over others will use any tool to spread hate, and then even God becomes an unwilling part in it. The fact that He didn't empower or guide them to commit such horror is lost, and so, to those who don't know better, God is seen to be a part of the problem when they claim their victory.

When Jesus was my spirit guide, at my request, he gave me a prayer to help turn people away from terrorism, saying:

'It has pursued a career of upsetting proportions, through the efforts of those who create mayhem and upset through a love of evil.

For they're not displaying God's Love, and it's a hopeless task to expect a man to feel at ease with the need for a weapon in his hand. Yet he has the option to put it down and walk away. I ask now that he finds the need to resist all anger and use the power within as a basis of love instead.'

You can see that he emphasises that ***the organisers of terrorism have a desire for perpetuating evil***, and that the people they groom to commit such tragedies, do have a choice whether to go through with them, or simply walk away.

Speaking Personally, I remember doubting that this prayer would have an effect. But soon after he gave it to me, a 'would be terrorist' did refuse to set off a bomb, and I realised that, the more of us who said the prayer, the stronger the forces would be to deter these individuals. So please join me.

The Foundation of Life

At the moment terrorism and war remain ever-present threats, and where there's hurt and a level of ignorance, there are controlling powers who will feed them evil, while many innocents continue to experience the pain of their authority.

But the human race can be indomitable if it chooses, and this is the point where the strength of the people must loudly voice its need to develop peace and cooperation, so that the world can find its true power again. And it's here where we can begin this.

When we look at the formula for life, its foundation includes one massively powerful constant, and that is God. As you work through this book, I will introduce you to various aspects of this omnipotent Spirit Being that show the true value of His Power.

So, whether or not you already believe in God, this incredible Spirit Energy does exist, and God won't leave the scene even if you do still doubt Him.

The Energies That Surround Us.

Just as we are surrounded by the air we breathe, similarly we are surrounded by our own, and many other spirit energies. Like air, you may not see them as you get on with your day, but if you learn to relax your eyes at times, you may see a brightness around people, trees, and other living things and that is an aura/energy.

When you grow more able to do this, you can be rewarded with an amazing rainbow of colours at times, that can reflect the health of each living person, animal, and object through its inner vibrancy. There is a movement of energy around us as people, and even around plants and trees, as well as the planet itself.

The energies that trees have are powerful, and that's an important part of the vibrancy that exists within the world, so you can understand why there are Elementals such as Fairy and Elf energies that help to maintain their strengths and keep them as disease free as is possible. We must value all of them more.

Add to the picture the energies of the spirit helpers that deliver God's Power, to maintain and adjust as necessary the vibrancy here on Earth, and you can realise that you're really a small, but integral, part of a much larger system of life than is apparent. But although each of us is a very small cog in a huge wheel, if there's a problem with just one of those cogs it will reverberate throughout the whole system, and so it is with the planet and even beyond.

God's Wisdom

As I was told in July 2021 in a writing, God's Wisdom is precious to us all, whether or not we admit to it in our life here on Earth. Its vibrancy is vital to our organs, and those of every living being on the planet. It's there to be of immense value to everyone and should be accepted as such, because without it we are underpowered.

When we respond positively to God's Power it allows us to progress and that in turn allows change to happen. In fact, with each level we evolve to, it brings us closer to the Godhead, and allows us greater strength, and understanding for the future and all that that can bring with it.

Programmer Extraordinaire

We can so easily take for granted our lives and the world around us, but if you marvel at the programmers who deliver such amazing technology, and data for us to use on computers and phones, then consider God, because this amazingly Powerful Spirit Energy is the Ultimate Programmer.

He is 'Programmer Extraordinaire' dealing with all the intricacies of each and every life on the planet, and helping them to bond, and bring opportunities for us to learn and develop in a positive way.

It's true that in some ways mankind has reached amazing levels, but in every way God surpasses their achievements many times over, and not just here on Earth.

God's Role within the Universe

Back in 2011 God spoke within my writings of being the Spirit Being that serves planets within this Universe. But He also added that possibly at some point He would be called on to serve planets outside it.

He said that by bringing life it allows a planet to develop in a way of belief, which then makes it sacred, and He added that it brings a greater value if the life is given purpose, which can then direct the thinking of its inhabitants.

When you consider that paragraph, you can see that there are four key parts to the success of the formula for a healthy planet. They are belief, a sacred planet, value, and purpose.

I think that at the moment we must ask:
- Do we view our planet as sacred?
- Does our race have a strong enough belief?
- Has our vision of value changed from God's version?
- Does humankind live with true purpose?

God went on to tell me that the higher powers within the Universe call on His help to do the work of creation, and support. These powers are from various planets, and they've worked tirelessly to format other ones over many years.

Just as we would expect with an organised business, these higher powers bring their resolution to God, the Source and then they call on Him to begin the work of Creation. But this isn't a decision made with only a business head, because they're also at His side to understand and then define in a compassionate way, a better future for each planet to build towards.

In fact, God said that as they are a force of great intellect, they are recognised as a vital stand in the power of ecological preparation, adding

'Ask if I am happy to be alongside such Beings of worth, and I can accurately say that they are of incredible stature and power themselves; and that they have a hallowed thinking towards the power needed to bring about a valued and worthwhile planet.'

He went on to say that He serves because of their authority, and solely with the need to bring the might and purpose of God's values to the forefront of such thinking.

He then referred particularly to planet Earth, saying that in that way, He can commit to the growth and worth needed to bring about essential changes that can save the human race from devaluing the world, and bringing more upset to an already open wound.

He finished by saying that He asks for the authority to do more than just support, and because of that He felt He should explain His part in this work.

More Detail on God's Role

As a Creator, God brings a vital spark to a young child after it's born. Their growth is gentle at first, so that they can bring about a need for life, and develop the wisdom needed to walk, and also manipulate hands, fingers, and the rest.

Once the infant is old enough, God brings the need to grow a better balance in the way that a growing child needs, but once they are adult, they can use their own will to bring change, and when other people's authority is also mixed in, life becomes more puzzling and maybe even compromising.

God has the power to intervene and elect that that child will grow in a balanced way according to His guidelines. But the overall need is to learn, so if that young adult has a need to learn about goodness, the ingredients are there for that to be achievable.

Of course, life doesn't always follow a good direction, and if their journey plan requires them to have a harrowing or upsetting time, then that too is given. (So much depends on what challenges that person's soul chose to experience)

However, there must be a freedom of choice, and when that person recognises God's Presence, it can become a more powerful and worthwhile life as a whole.

But having said that, some young people do end up being guided or even misguided by their peers, parents and others who are on their own journeys, and when that happens it can bring disappointment. So, living by the Worth of God is a powerful journey to take, but other people's interference can be enough to turn them away from focusing on good, and instead point them in an upsetting direction and failure.

Chapter Three: Spirit Realms and Forces

Including: The Spirit Realms; Guiding Roles; Death On Earth And Your Spirit's Return Home; Souls With Behavioural Problems; Lower Levels Of The Spirit Realms; The Lowest Level Of The Spirit Realms; The Support Available On Earth; Speaking Personally; Help Comes In Different Ways; Help Is Always Available Through Our Spirit Helpers; Speaking Personally; **When** *Folklore Meets The 21st Century; When Belief Defeats Modern Logic; A Working Spirit Team; Joining The Team; Angels And Fairies Work Together; The Work Of Fairies; The Work Of Elves; Helping Fairies; Speaking Personally; The Power Of Planet Earth; Humanity's Attitude To Earth; Understand Evil; Learn About Evil; The Devil, Lucifer, Satan And Demons; The Elemental Roles Of Dwarves, Goblins, And Gnomes.*

The Spirit Realms

My writings from spirit have brought me an amazing insight into life this side of the veil and beyond to the afterlife.

In 2009, Jesus told me that the sheer simplicity of the Spirit Realms surprises some returning souls, because its immense peace generates goodness. In fact all those who call it 'Home' feel at ease there.

The many levels within the Spirit Realms also make it a worthwhile place for all those remaining within it. So, even though those souls returning from their life on Earth still equate in some ways with the needs of those they left behind, they immediately feel at home.

The Realms serve many needs. It's both a home to spirit, as well as being a tranquil place for the souls that need some respite after their life on Earth.

Added to that, it's a place of learning, serving many souls across the different levels of understanding. It delivers knowledge to those who need to learn about the future, and because they're at peace with themselves, it shows them how to bring authority to their learning; perfect timing as you would expect, as they've reached a point in their development, where they're ready for that. The challenges of Earth are no longer there, so they're content to learn anything that can bring them greater understanding for the future.

It really is impossible to pass through the Spirit Realms without gaining some knowledge; but still, simplicity is the keyword. Those, who applied the law on Earth, find that there's only one authority needed in the Realms, and that's given by God and comes from the heart. Everyone must abide by it. There's no need to caution or punish anyone, and there's nothing to fear there, because those in the world of spirit are at peace with it, and they're able to counteract all evil through the spirit mind, which is something that everyone is comfortable with.

Guiding Roles

As our own lives unfold over many eras and ages, we do acquire an impressive knowledge, which allows us to equate with the needs of younger spirits.

So, a rule of passage was established long ago that each soul that has learned from an Earthly life, will in turn help another soul who has begun a life on Earth, and in that way the development can continue. For we are each sent to Earth to learn the practicality of living an embodied experience. That then enables us to understand the issues that humanity faces. But inevitably, we all wonder about that part of our life that draws us back from

Earth to our spirit home, and as God expanded greatly on that, I think you'll find this interesting.

Death On Earth And Your Spirit's Return Home

Very little has been said about the soul's return home to the Spirit Realms, but in 2014, God gave me these details to share with you.

He began by saying that when a person dies on Earth they're given healing at the outset on their journey through to the Spirit Realms.

He said that first, the soul is raised from the lifeless human body, and at that point, it experiences a new level of consciousness that enables it to understand its ability to survive and move on.

If it's been someone who suffered a lot on Earth, during the time that they were waiting to die, their body may have known aches and pains, or been consumed by some disease. But as soon as the spirit arrives in the Spirit Realms, they're given the healing that frees them of that. So suddenly, they feel alert and active, and that can help them to feel capable of moving on again. That's necessary because they need to develop in the way God has planned for them.

That means that if in the past they failed to act where needed, they may have a period of reform, or possibly focus on developing past abilities. Whatever it is, spirit has everything there so that they can grow further.

It may sound rather harsh that there's no time to relax and ignore development for a while, but in truth, it's a good situation, because a person's spirit is able to lift quickly, and it can take on new and vital areas of power within a few days (in human terms) of that person's death on Earth.

The only upset within a soul is where it carries the results of unwise choices on Earth, or there are certain character changes. Where they occur, they must be dealt with differently.

That's because those energies have come from the Earth Plane. They may have brought an unforgiving energy to both the brain and soul, and that causes an inertness within the soul, that blocks its need to move on.

If it's a serious upset their spirit may need to wait for a new life on Earth, to clear some of the actual ill within the soul. This will be achieved by a regression therapist who will then work to remove such blockages from a person's soul, and once that's done it frees it of past impediments.

Another situation that occurs is when the soul has gained an attitude of contempt. That brings about a different type of inertness, and the soul must then spend some time on an 'Attitude Plane' within the Spirit Realms, because that has to be remedied before the soul is able to gain momentum again and continue its journey with ardour and purpose.

There are also many people who defined a career of upset during their time on Earth, and when they return to the Spirit Realms, first of all they must **regain the need** to move forward strongly and powerfully, before they can embark on the particular type of healing that then allows them to progress.

That's because the development path is prohibited to all those, who have a derisive attitude or have wielded the type of power that made others suffer during their time on Earth. There's an area devoted to those souls, and they are unable to move on until they have healed their attitude; the reason being that they must learn awareness and gain new light for their direction. To bring about a change of attitude they must allow that light to shine on the darkness that is there within their soul's character, and ensure they no longer feel derisory or have a need to develop upset.

Lower Levels Of The Spirit Realms

As you can see, the lower parts of the Spirit Realms are remedial levels for those who abused their time on Earth, however, they're not within the lowest and worst plane. That's because although they've lost their need for joy and purpose in their life, they haven't actually felt the need to bring horror and upset so great that it can only be seen as the greatest evil.

The Lowest Level Of The Spirit Realms

For those who do qualify for the lowest plane, they must serve time within the confines of what can only be described as a living hell, because it confines the spirit to a level of inert behaviour that doesn't allow the soul to move forward at all.

It carries within that Realm a horrible fear of inertness because it grinds down the character of upset in order to reveal, at a point where it's possible, a way forward of purpose and attitude. That can then motivate a power within the spirit to do well, and actually resolve the upset within them. But, to reach that point that soul must first complete a time of inertness.

In order to be of value again, that soul must be brought back from its need to bring such horror and upset, and move to a place where it can again value the life given to it. So, dictators and others who use their own version of threats and upset on Earth, follow this direction on their return to the Spirit Realms because, instead of a path of true development, they followed a taste for devastation and killing.

God explained that their need on Earth was to be god and added that He could see within these people that their belief was that by bringing distress and pain they could actually bring value to a divisive world.

But as God points out, no worthwhile god can remain true to the world while at the same time violating it, and that God's need is to bring love and good, so upset has no value. It's worthless.

But He said that those who defy the rules are blind to that, because they can't allow themselves to be seen as anything less than powerful; and that doesn't bode well for the world, or for them when they eventually return to the Spirit Realms.

He ended by saying that development is there for us at all viable points of our journey, and that includes the challenging time that we spend on Earth, where there are numerous spirit helpers, but they're not always recognised.

It's important to know that those who hurt others, are themselves punished, and God explained it in this way.

He said that the souls that are subject to the Laws of the Universe, receive sufficient upset to turn around their thinking and values.

This may be within the disturbing area of the lower levels of the Spirit Realms, or it may be given in the harsh discipline of another life, where all the pain and upset they have caused is brought back on them in a form of karma.

If the hurt they have caused is minor, they may serve time in the base levels of the Spirit Realms or be kept on one where they can no longer inflict upset on anyone.

But when they've brought actual cruelty, the soul finds itself within the lowest level of the Spirit Realms, and it endures so much upset that it actually brings a fear of existing. That continues until it's finally found to be compatible with a journey of growth. However, this may take the equivalent of many human years.

There's also a punishment that comes directly from God, and that's for those who abuse the Name or Purpose of God in some way.

If a person has impacted on the Worth of God they're left in a void, and barren place until the time when they're fit and able to further their journey of growth.

However, there's no direct call for God to impede a life, unless that person has in some way diminished the highest values to which God adheres.

The Support Available on Earth

The writings that I receive from these powerful beings repeat again and again that even though life on Earth has the potential to achieve so much, the human race is now so disturbed that it *cannot* fulfil a role of true authority.

That's why every person on Earth is given a team of spirit helpers who will throughout that person's life, be there to help them fulfil their needs for authority, guidance, security and worth; and these are your team of angels, elementals, and spirit guides.

The problem is that many people here on Earth don't call on their help, either because they're not aware that it exists, or that it carries such authority.

Yet they should, because there are so many ways they can be helped, which would diminish heartache and secure a better future for everyone.

Some of the information I'm given refers to the increasing number of lawyers and politicians in the world and says that the human race has misplaced its authority to bring about changes, and that has not improved the world, but instead has made it a forbidding place. So, it doesn't enhance people's lives, but instead takes away from them. and that mustn't continue.

There are also many laws and upsets caused by politicians, who have the authority to make wise choices but don't.

Instead, there's a hierarchy of lawmakers who feel pleased with themselves when they implement new laws to which everyone must conform. Yet, many people would respond better to a 'please' or 'thank you' instead of yet another law that they have no choice but to obey.

In truth, those in positions of power should learn from God.

For God is the authority, from which we can learn to rule our lives without the threat of anarchy or upset. And if we are to restore quality to life as a whole, we must realise that love is the healing energy and not force.

Speaking Personally. Surely life on Earth would be better if we focused on preventing problems rather than waiting for them to happen and then punishing those who break the laws?

On the other side, those who make laws rarely experience the same conditions and pressures that many minor lawbreakers do, so they have little understanding and possibly limited interest in what leads someone to commit a crime. Their perspective is so different.

A few years ago, when I counselled a lifer in prison, I learned there was a high percentage of young offenders that were illiterate.

Having dodged school, when they applied for a job, they found they couldn't complete the application form and that's the point where they looked for other ways to get money, and another teenager would find that life could be unforgiving.

Help Comes in Different Ways

There are a few inspired people who use their own skills, time and understanding to coach and mentor the young, and they channel their energies and enthusiasm in valuable and positive ways. Can that action be replicated?

Similarly, preventing a released offender from reoffending is important and by offering longer support than at present, it would surely channel funding in a more positive way. New laws don't necessarily solve the problems.

Help Is Always Available Through Our Spirit Helpers

Your eyes may only see the physical forms on Earth, but if you add all the available spirit forms in their physical state, almost every corner of the world would be as busy as Time Square on New Year's Eve, and we'd be totally distracted. We'd achieve nothing.

So, having spirit energies around us but unseen, allows a certain distancing, whilst we enjoy the guidance and empowerment of amazing beings who help us to achieve the goals we seek.

Once you accept all the energies that affect your life on Earth you realise that there's a complex formula that makes life work; rather like the swan gliding regally along the surface of the water, while below it's a busier picture.

Our human society comprises of people with various abilities and skills, and the angelic and elemental levels of energy vary similarly to support *their* roles.

There are different levels of angels. Each specialises in different life needs There are other books that go into more detail about them, so here I'll only talk briefly about archangels and angels.

Despite these beings holding a widely accepted religious link through Zoroastrianism, Judaism Christianity, and Islam, I use these names to simply identify the roles between spirit beings.

When you need guidance or empowerment of some type, who do you ask? Angels? Archangels? Fairies? Elves? Your Spirit Guide? There's a very simple option. Ask God for help. To contact any part of the Team your request passes through God's Energy, and then that help will come from the one that's best suited to your need. God sees the big picture, therefore His judgement is always better than ours. So don't stress, just go to the Expert!

Many years ago, Jesus told me that the angel is a spectacular creature of great light and beauty. But such an entrancing being can help you with very practical stuff at times. The angel is wise beyond understanding.

Have you ever asked Angels to find you a parking place in a busy area? They do and it can help save you a lot of stress. Ask before you arrive there, and your day may flow better.

There are many Angels within the world, determined to help. Their love is for all people, and they work together to instigate changes that can counteract poverty, shame, and upset. If needed, they'll bring happiness to your day as well as the inner strength to make changes in your life.

They'll nurture you, so you don't feel a failure, but instead understand why you need to grow. However, you first need to develop that relationship. Don't hesitate. It's a win, win situation.

They're a happy, generous force that work within the Will of God, to create changes in the world, in a way that brings authority and stability for the future, and they can help you in many ways because they're amazingly powerful. Their purpose is not to deviate or upset you, unless in specific circumstances where they are told to by God; but even then it's only to bring about a good and stable effect for your planned life journey.

Your Guardian Angel acts as a restraint against those who may otherwise obstruct you on your path, but they're not the one, who protects you most in life, because they're only there to do God's Will at specified times.

Other Angels come to your defence when needed in a battle or beyond. They work in many dimensions, so one will always be there to protect you from harm.

When it comes to the day-to-day things, you *can* ask the Angels for help, because those are often the issues that will throw your day off balance, or stress you, and when you're aware of them, those feelings of guidance can keep you safe.

Archangels are God's Messenger Force. Sometimes the world needs a boost, and Archangels have the best way of delivering that.

They can overcome evil, and they're valuable whenever and wherever they're needed, working out there in the Galaxy as well as here on Earth, and each of them is a force with the ability to bring change to your life.

Imagine you're learning how to handle a particular level of success or deal with a failure. Either way, you must be completely effective in what you do. But the Archangels are around you day and night, bringing God's Power to you. So, ask God, and it will be given.

Jesus once told me that they will still be there at the end of time, when there is no more evil to be had, and only good. This is their formula, the one for good, and they'll always be there as God's force against evil.

But just remember that it's **you who** has free choice in how you use the power that's given to you. Neither God nor the Archangels make your decisions for you! You may focus on the trust you have to place on God and the spirit helpers, but they also have to trust you to fulfil your given tasks.

First, the Archangels test your initiative, and then they balance out the best way to act, in order that it allows that power to be seen and felt.

The role of the Spirit Guides was brought about so that a more mature spirit could guide a younger one, and it's unique to this planet. When a member of the human race becomes a Spirit Guide, they no longer return to live a life on Earth.

God has said that later there will be no need for the role of Spirit Guide, but we've not reached that point yet.

It's part of the mechanism of spirit power that's often unrecognised. But whether or not you do acknowledge them, they exist, and to an extent, you can say the same about all the helpers within God's Team. Your choice is whether you wish to learn about them and act on their wisdom.

Let me emphasise that this isn't about 'talking to dead people'! They're as alive as you or I. They're just actively alive on a different plane. Just think of it as standing downstairs and calling to someone upstairs. Maybe you can't see them, but just know that they're there!

Whether or not you choose to take notice of them, Spirit Guides are part of your life. They can bring yet another strength to your day, and I think that's always welcome. But you don't have to have a conversation with them. Just acknowledge that they're there, and work with that enhanced power and understanding.

Life is more than simply existing from day to day. Our lives are multi-dimensional and along with those daily needs, we all face many decisions that affect our health, our mood, and our emotional state, as well as the development of our spirit, so we all benefit when we're helped through the demands of our day.

We're not robots, and as life stands now we need mental support, and inspired vision; we look for a feeling of fulfilment which comes from achievement. We also need to be reassured now and then that we're on the right path, and that we're doing a good job.

I mean, who hasn't crashed and felt a complete failure? But God has taken that into account, and so when you do it's the point where a Spirit Guide will be there as you pick yourself up, and they'll help you realise that with a little more focus, you'll achieve that elusive goal. Their skill lies in the fact that they've known situations in their own time on Earth that demanded similar life skills to both endure and win through the bad times.

They're not just picked from the 'crowd'; they're matched to your needs. They've already developed the skills to overcome or survive what you're currently going through. So, when difficulties arise, they'll be there to bring their support and wisdom.

Your main Spirit Guide is a positive asset to your life, and if you develop to a point where their skills are no longer relevant, a new guide will step in to help you through the next issues you face.

That doesn't mean that there's only one. Support may also come from close relatives and friends who are now in spirit. They bring their love and support as appropriate.

Each day, you face the guiding influence of parents, teachers, tutors, managers, and others in your life, and while some of that help is useful, other influences may propose what they would choose for themselves, rather than what is appropriate to you and your needs. So be careful what you follow. Go with your gut feeling.

It's safe to say that life's targets are better achieved with the specialist help and support that God can put in your direction through the Angels, the Elementals and also your Spirit Guides. Remember too, that your guidance may direct you towards skilled help here on Earth if that is what you need. Once that happens you're in the area of specialists for which there's no substitute.

Spirit Guides can range from great leaders to slaves, but that doesn't mean that one is powerful, and the other isn't. It's the strengths in their character and attitude that helped them deal with that role.

A slave can be very powerful in a different way. They had to be focused and determined in their belief in order to survive cruelty. They also had to be strong mentally, physically, and emotionally to exist through a time of bondage.

Any true leader will have to have shown understanding and also learned compassion within his qualities of leadership. Both these examples may have had their own Spirit Guides to help them through their own development.

So, in short, whether or not you know who your main guide is, you can be assured that the right powers are working around you and with you at every point in your life. But they can only help you to succeed if you *act* on their positive guidance.

Why would we turn our backs on such valuable help? A closed mind? An arrogant attitude?

Speaking Personally, any true leader will have to have shown understanding and also learned compassion within his qualities of leadership. Look at the example set by Nelson Mandela. I have listened to a past MI6 agent call him a terrorist. But following the terrorism came a humbling through his incarceration. He would have had spirit influencers to help him see a different power, because the man brought together the hearts, souls, and minds of enemies and helped them live with more tolerance on a world stage. He certainly inspired me.

When Folklore Meets The 21st Century

I know that some of you may laugh uncontrollably at the thought of Fairies at the bottom of your garden, but it's the seed of truth that brings life to a lot of folklore. And if you need to work more efficiently, or your garden has many trees, you may have Elves too!

Consider that Planet Earth/ Gaia is also a living being, and you will realise that there is a whole parcel of life wrapped up in our planet. As well as responding to the many positives and negatives aimed at it, its energies have always been a support to the many lives here that call it 'home'.

It's true that the Earth has an energy that we take too much for granted. In truth we don't appreciate our planet enough. It's simply become part of the package; basically, something to stand on, which provides areas of beauty as well as areas to dump stuff we don't want any more! Truly, we have degraded Earth in so many ways, that it now fights for survival.

I'll only touch briefly on the existence of Elementals because it's a big subject, and to be honest, I just need you to be aware that they ***do*** exist. They're part of the overall team, in fact, an important part.

Some are no longer here because the human race has developed a toxic world with its material aims and attitude to war and power, and ultimately, the control that accompanies it; so diverse energies like Pixies and Unicorns now belong firmly in the past.

Those that do commonly exist include:

Fairies, Elves, Nature Spirits, Water Sprites, Imps, Gnomes, Goblins and more. Leprechauns have gone into hiding, because of the many negative energies within the world, but when that improves, hopefully they too will become more apparent.

Gnomes, Dwarves, and Goblins are the three Elementals that belong to the team of evil beings. JK Rowling captured the Goblin's character fairly accurately in her Harry Potter books, but I'm afraid that the friendly Gnomes in so many gardens belie the truth. If you see a real one, then that's because you're already involved in low energy dealings. Having said that, they're all integral working parts within the massive jigsaw we call 'Life on Earth'.

Fortunately, even in the 21st century, some people's awareness about these Earth beings is stronger than might be expected.

When Belief Defeats Modern Logic

As recently as 2013, believers in Elves, together with environmentalists, urged authorities in Iceland to abandon a highway project that they claimed would disturb Elf habitat, including an Elf church.

The project was halted until the supreme court of Iceland ruled on the case brought by the 'Friends of

Lava' who had cited both the impact on the environment, and the detrimental effect on Elf culture if the road project went through. The positive result was that the construction had to wait until the Elves, known in Iceland as the 'Hidden folk or the Huldufolk' had moved on to a safe area.

Some may laugh scornfully at that, but the truth is that we must open our eyes and minds to the fact that life really does include many different powerful energies, and that they deal daily with different imbalances that affect plant life, animal life, our lives and of course the Planet's.

We have a habit of believing that if we can't see something then it doesn't exist, but that's far from the truth.

A Working Spirit Team

Those who recognise Gaia (the Planet Earth) rather than God, readily understand the presence and power of the Elementals, but generally 'that world' and the 'religious' one remain in completely separate camps.

So, it hardly seems possible that the Being that the Christian Faith recognises correctly as the Son of God was the One who taught me about this fascinating and powerful section of spirit help.

Jesus went into more detail than I can here, and it helped me to understand that just as we have people like doctors, nurses, farmers, veterinarians, and others to look after areas of our lives, these small but powerful energies each have their own specialist areas of work in the flora and fauna, and even with us.

Angels, Fairies, Elves, and other Elementals may seem an unlikely grouping, but they all come under one banner...God's Banner. Just as God created the Angels, the Angels created the Fairies/ Earth Angels, so they all work together well.

God is Host to all these energies, but along with this team, you will see that I also include the Planet Earth itself, because it truly has its own powerful energy that can boost your inner force, and work to sustain life.

It works with the energies that are given by God directly and through God's Team. However, as a living planet, it's also affected each day by the strengths of good and bad committed by us, the human population. So, when we nurture the planet and spread goodness throughout the world it does well, but for a long time now, we have taken riches from the Earth, and dumped toxic rubbish in its place. In other ways too we threaten its survival each day, and the result is that it's growing sick and weaker.

We share Earth with so many beings, who were here long before we came, and indeed, they're constantly adjusting in order to bring about a better formula for the future. Mankind of course takes credit for many changes in the world. It prefers to believe it's in control, while behind the scenes, the Elementals and Angels are adjusting and balancing to compensate for our poor decisions.

Joining The Team

Jesus said that although God will bring about many necessary changes in order that the world moves on, it can't happen without our help, working where necessary to clear up the mess humanity's created, so that the world as a whole can progress to a better future.

The Angelic Realm has been the sector of spirit help that's brought many changes in the need to avert disaster, and it's mostly with them that we all work, as they're the ones who bring about the needed goodness to the world, where it's lacking.

But we do also need to thank all the Elementals that work together, because they manifest good, by bringing about values that resonate with God. It's interesting that they ask nothing in return. They're simply happy to give their best, and then receive the confirmation that all's well within the world.

Angels And Fairies Work Together

Some Angels work closely with Fairies because together they act as a team to bring about change.

Combating illness is one important concept to both Angels and Fairies, so they bring together their powers to ease suffering wherever they can. However, if a patient *needs to* learn from their illness, then they combine their powers in order to anticipate the usual distress caused by it, and help everyone who's involved to overcome the inevitable sadness and upset that can follow.

But that's where it can be difficult because some people, who are ill or anticipate being so, sometimes lose faith and shut themselves off from God's help, and when that happens, the Angels and Fairies are unable to deliver that valuable aid.

Those individuals may believe that God hasn't answered their prayers to recover, but if that wasn't in the blueprint, when their life was planned, and dying from a disease or other illness was a chosen experience, God is unable to change that. Yet, with the understanding that He is still present, prayers can instead ask for the strength to cope with what's ahead, and that can be very empowering.

The Work of Fairies

All in all, Fairies want you to be a happy person with a love for life, and so they try to make it easier for you, by releasing the energies that made you sad and bringing forward more compatible ones that fit with the need to be happy. Allow it and it'll happen for you.

The countryside is rich with Fairies but there are also some in the cities that help keep parks and smaller gardens better for nature.

So, it's essential to generate faith in the Fairies, because they work tirelessly to develop a better environment, even down to composting and saving on waste.

They can do a lot to help the countryside, and if farmers grow hemp (the non-toxic variety) in a corner of a field it'll help Fairies immensely, as they can then use it to stimulate the field's growth. Hemp is a plant that has a lot of uses, and it'll also bring about better digestion for all grazing animals, if it's used in their feed.

Many Fairies inhabit the world, working to serve humanity's needs to the best of their ability, they can't undo our wrongs; and so, they work with us to help remedy them.

They have an obligation to bring about change in humankind as a whole in order for it to reach a new level of understanding, and they fulfil God's requirement. But that can only happen when humanity rediscovers the need to gain knowledge and be worthwhile in the world.

Fairies can bring some astonishing thoughts that will develop your calibre and personal value, so ask for their help, and that'll bring magic to your life, as they can see what's needed.

When you allow them, they'll help you to discern between good and evil, and they'll also help you to trust and make quicker decisions. That's because they can stimulate changes in your attitude, and format strength and determination.

So let go of that childish picture in your mind. We're talking here about an elemental that possesses great skills, and just as they can help you to develop your own, you can repay Fairies by helping them to be completely worthwhile to the planet's needs.

The Work of Elves

Elves are quite different, and their help comes in another way.

It's the sort that allows you to achieve a variety of things, but in a more worthwhile way.

Many people are utterly bemused by the thought that an Elf could benefit them, but in truth, their intense power can help you to bring things to a conclusion where it would totally defeat others.

They're definitely there to help you, but they don't settle for any result short of the best. Failure is out of the question!

So why not ask them for help on your next project?

It's simple enough, because they're waiting for your communication, and just like any team, you only need to put in a request and then they'll be there.

It must be vital stuff though, otherwise they won't be interested.

Having said that, the more difficult the problem, the more help you'll receive.

But it's not just effort that's necessary. They look for proper planning, so that they can respond with a dynamic approach.

If you're just doing simple stuff then, you're on your own.

Helping Fairies

Believe it or not, you can help Fairies in a very simple and practical way in your own garden, and it's also a nice way to introduce children into working with these precious Elementals.

Simply ensure there's clean water available for them to drink, and some shelter for rest. Many Fairies rely on water within the garden, even if it's only in a bucket or a plant holder; water is a drink that helps provide light, as well as a regenerative factor in their appearance so that it makes them visible to the bees and butterflies, as well as all the other insects that pollinate plants.

Fairies can only bring about change if it's a happy garden. That may sound strange, but if it's ridden with chemicals, and many insects and plants are dying, it's difficult for fairies to attain a high level of production, for they're used to working with natural forces, and unnatural ones can only harm them, because they're not given the right conditions to work in.

They also need somewhere to rest that's away from the heart of the work, and they relax and take naps so that afterwards, they can work to bring about whatever changes are needed; so, ensure that there's some shelter for them. Fairies never sleep but they do rest in a way that allows them to restore their energies fully, and that's necessary, as they work to help restore Planet Earth's strength.

Speaking Personally, I've found sometimes that as a race, we focus on details that spirit don't necessarily see as important.

I remember when Jesus was my guide that I asked how to spell a name he'd given. He told me that spelling wasn't important.

Another thing we like to do is identify all the spirit help we have around us. We want a name for the Angels, Fairies, Elves, and whoever else is helping us. Maybe it brings us a feeling of closeness, and yet they are close anyway.

Spirit guides may automatically give us their names. White Cloud introduced himself in his first writing to me, and yet Jesus refused to for almost three weeks, because he rightly said that some people are so interested in who their guide is, that they don't listen to the message. Isn't that the case?

But it became a part of one of my day courses, that once everyone had contacted their spirit helper they then asked their name, so that they could talk to them at times.

A few years ago, at my course in Harrogate on the last day of February, everyone was focusing to find out the name of the Elf who was working with them that day.

They'd already named the Fairies, and again using their awareness they in turn told me the names of their Elves.

'Edward' was the first name given by one lady. Not very Elflike you may think!

I moved to the next woman, she smiled and said, 'Robert, but they call me Bob'.

Suddenly, I realised what was happening.

True, they were providing a name by which to recognise them, but they were also using my father's names. His name was Robert Edward, but everyone called him Bob, and it was pertinent because the following day was the anniversary of his passing to the Spirit Realms. So, it was a poignant moment as their choices had brought him closer to me that afternoon.

So, remember that names aren't always necessary, but a 'thank you' definitely is!

The Power Of Planet Earth

I'll only touch briefly here on this subject, as you'll find many other books that will bring more detail than I can commit to here.

Gaia is the ancient Greek name given by those who worship the Earth as the Prime Energy Being. In mythology she was the Mother Goddess presiding over the planet. Many Neo-pagans worship Gaia, but although the Earth is powerful this belief dismisses the presence of God, so once again it isn't providing a complete picture.

But when you slot in these pieces of the jigsaw not only with the Elementals, but also the Angels and most importantly God, you're moving towards a more complete representation, for although Earth has a hugely important power, it doesn't work in isolation, and God told me years ago that *He* is the Host of All Energies.

Humanity's Attitude To Earth

In the past, there's been an assumption by the human race that the Planet would provide its unique richness for always, and that it would not need or receive anything in return. So, it has taken more and more from the planet and depleted its strength.

When we did start giving back, it wasn't then in a good way. Our 'gifts' have been dangerous radiation, chemicals, damaging vibrations from warfare, mountains of rubbish, an overload of negativity, and a total lack of care or conscience.

So, the world as a whole is damaged, and now it's our task to begin the big job of healing, because we can't afford to put it off. Late, but not yet too late we are learning that this Planet is a vital force and it's an integral part of life's jigsaw.

Understand Evil

Evil Spirit Beings working within the Earth plane include The Devil, Satan, Lucifer, and Demons. Evil Earthbound Spirit Beings include such Elementals as Dwarves, Gnomes and Goblins. Each has a role to fulfil.

The Peril of Evil

Our lives here on Earth provide us with free will, which means that our choices are our own, and although guidance is available to us, we are still free to formulate our life in the way that we decide, allowing for outside influences that may also colour our choices along the way.

So, do we choose to take the good path, or the evil one?

Well, life provides both and each one brings its own lessons. But of course, there will be many of those decisions to make, and if you're not sharpening your senses, a lot of opportunities are there to confuse or persuade you into taking the wrong direction.

There's so much that's unclear about the roles of Evil Spirits. Religion has brought misleading information particularly about Satan, and I especially want to correct this.

I want to share vital information that I received from Jesus in 2009, when he acted as my main spirit guide, and it answers so many questions. I talked earlier about the lower levels of the Spirit Realms, and its representation of Hell. Now I want to provide details about the three **main** beings that we recognise as representing Evil i.e. The Devil, Lucifer, and Satan.

Again, so much confusion lies in who is who, and generally Satan is blamed for most things, so you may be very surprised when I tell you that he actually works within the knowledge and purpose of God. So let me explain more.

The Devil, Lucifer, Satan, And Demons

There are three forces of evil here, but as you'll see there are huge differences in their roles.

Jesus explained that the **Devil's** aim is to create sorcery and upset to the world in a cruel way that brings a need to restore good and worth again where there's damage.

This evil being is there to deliver a level of apathy and a feeling of powerlessness.

Negativity is sadly rife in the world as we are all encouraged to focus on what is wrong, rather than appreciating the good that is here for us all. So, when humankind requires this authority, the Devil delivers it, together with the wrath and all the upsets.

He's expert on being devious, unkind, and hateful, and he brings these to the door of anyone who shows the need for it.

Protagonists and war are brought to the fore. It's his forte, and he can develop as much evil as he needs by causing mayhem.

The Devil's stamp is evil, and with that authority he takes any of those who don't use their abilities to generate good.

As we have seen in information about the lowest level in the Spirit Realms, when the person targeted by the Devil dies, their soul doesn't revert to evil within that Hell, but is instead thwarted at every turn, in order to bring about the good again.

There are, in fact, many ways the soul can be impeded by the Devil if needed. He's resolute, and it'll take the Grace of God to completely cleanse the soul again, to allow growth, because if it's not thorough it will not be completely safe.

So, they remain in the lowest levels within the Spirit Realms until their soul conforms to good again, and they are able once more to continue their journey of development.

Lucifer is a separate being to the Devil.

His beginnings were as a man who actually lived as the Devil decreed, and then became a fallen angel in the way that he was human form, but had come to Earth as an angel, who asked to learn the knowledge of mankind.

He became Lucifer when he developed as a messenger for the Devil's work, in order to achieve notoriety. He's someone from the past who became known for his evil deeds.

This didn't happen without help and it was the Devil who fuelled his desire.

So now he's lost to mankind and will only reveal himself to those who are closest to the Devil…his disciples.

He lives in the depths of upset, which you'll know as Hades, or by its other more common name, Hell, and from this risky path, we learn that he's now of immense value to the Devil, because he frees himself of any impediments, and walks freely among men in order to sanction upset wherever needed.

And so, we can now focus on a being whose role has been mistaken by so many.

I think Jesus' statement about **Satan** will surprise most people.

'Satan is led by goodness to bring a diversion and distress, but it's not to glorify upset, but to show its cruelty, and act as a catalyst for necessary change.'

There are so many situations that need changing in the world, and yet nothing is done. We may even have had the opportunity to influence some, but, like many people, we often make excuses and step back. Maybe as individuals, we feel it's outside our power to change things or it's someone else's responsibility, or the budget won't allow. It's then we stand back, and Satan takes over.

He creates something so terrible that we suddenly take the action that we should have done in the first place, and finally some good comes from the evil.

Yes, Satan is the catalyst and of course, the action results in suffering; that may be people, animals, or the environment, so it's learning at a high cost.

But willingly, or unwillingly, good must turn around the forces within the world and bring a positive change. It was achieved through an evil act, and Satan will have served God's good.

Some people believe that goodness only comes from God but there are some forces of good that also come from Satan; for he brings about change and raises a principle of values where offences have been committed.

Jesus told me that many people are daunted about the dark side of spiritual energy, but he said that it must be recognised that **demons** do in fact exist, and they will do evil if they need to. In fact, they won't be constrained if there's a lesson that needs to be learned.

So, we need to be alert to the strength of that evil because there's a heavy price to pay if we ignore the signs.

He said the role of Demons combines closely with the Devil, and that overall, there's a need to bring about change, so that the sordid world of upset and cruelty can be taken from the planet and released into a vacuum; a void where all apparent worth is lost, and it can release again the good in the world.

The Elemental Roles Of Dwarves, Goblins, And Gnomes,

Dwarves are really angry and troublesome, but having said that, they will actually help people to learn a lesson in right and wrong.

A dwarf is a defiant being who has skills of persuasion when a 'would be' petty criminal is resisting walking a better path, and really needs a taste of evil in order to realise where his or her mistakes can lead.

I must emphasise that we're not talking here about human beings, who were born with the condition of dwarfism. We're describing a small spirit elemental, who joins the realms of Goblins and Gnomes as a very unfriendly spirit creature.

Believe it or not, at one time the Goblin was a mellow creature, but in the 14th century crisis upon crisis hit countries throughout the world, because mankind was becoming more fraudulent and his lust for power was growing, so the Goblin changed tack, and began to create affrays which led to mayhem. This was to allow people to realise their wrongs and make amends, but they didn't, so the Goblin started making trouble, and bringing evil when change was needed.

At first that worked, but then a more menacing power grew in the world. People like Hitler, and Stalin believed they were above all rules, and could play God and dictate to the world.

In other situations, some yielded to the power of the Goblin force and made amends for their acts, but sadly many still continue to thwart the power of the Goblin today, in their need for wealth.

Last but not least I beg you not to be fooled by those cheery garden **Gnome** figures that show them as a friendly race.

Somewhere along the line they must have found a gullible advertising agent, because in real life, friendliness is far from their aim and they're to be avoided as they really do thrive on evil.

This being is table height and thrives on committing evil wherever there's an opportunity. Where there are low energies, low morals, crime, drugs, alcoholic overload and the rest, the not so friendly Gnome can be found.

But thankfully, the places you avoid are those where he thrives, so, you're not likely to share his company.

Chapter Four: Beyond Earth

Beyond Earth

Including: Other Planets; Similarities Between Planetary Races; Speaking Personally; Superior Intelligence Or Not; Let's Consider The Overall Picture; Abuhindra The Leader; Discussing The Youth Within The Planetary Races. Inhabited Planets Like Mars And Pluto; Lunar Power; Martians; Comparing Races And Purpose; The Power To Strengthen Other Planets; Esquaygo's Description Of Alubarium; The Diet And Humour On Alubarium; Speaking Personally; The Work Of Powers Within The Galaxy; Those Who Leave Their Planets To Heal Earth; Speaking Personally; When A Planet Is No Longer Habitable; The Power Of The Universe; Speaking Personally About Planetary Beings.

Other Planets

As our God also serves some other inhabited planets in this Galaxy, it's natural that we would want to know more about races that share the same Creator and support.

Also, to fully understand the potential of our planetary home we should look towards life beyond our own, because in many important ways, they hold a superior understanding.

Sadly, we're fed an overriding picture of hostile extraterrestrials through books and films, and with this potent portrayal of invaders, it's no wonder that's what becomes established in our minds. Straightaway it puts us on the offensive, and for as long as that remains, they'll not be able to communicate except with a few of us.

Through channelled information given by God, the Son of God and also certain communicating and powerful extraterrestrials, I can confirm that life definitely exists outside our own world. So, if logic is to be our lead, then Earth can't be the only planet with intelligent life within this or other Universes. And why would we want it to be unless it is to feed a growing arrogance. It would serve no practical purpose and life is certainly not a random happening. Great planning precedes all inhabited planets.

Similarities Between Planetary Races

A fascinating area of my channelled information has been about life on other planets. When Jesus was my Spirit Guide, he talked clearly about extraterrestrial life, and then God brought more information. Since that beginning, I have communicated directly with Esquaygo and currently much of my work is with Abuhindra.

I've been enthralled by their descriptions of life beyond our world, and amazed at the picture each of my guides have drawn about life outside our own, so maybe once you have read some of the detail given to me, you too will accept that beyond our own back yard we do have many intelligent neighbours.

My information speaks of beings on other planets who attend to their daily routines in a similar way to us, rising in the morning to greet the sun, and sleeping when their day is finished. Others live in underground cities, and don't know the light of day as we do here on Earth. Yet in other ways, I'm told that they're not dissimilar to us.

Just as in our world, life on other planets is devised by God, and it's based on the quantity and value of the oxygen and other gases filling the area above and around each one. The result is that in some instances, it's possible to grow a substance similar to the plants within our own atmosphere here on Earth, but for others it may only bring micro foods that are grown by delving deeper into the ground itself.

My information shows how there's a direct pattern between life on other planets with atmospheres like Earth's, but because the races on many of them have a greater awareness than we do, that does tend to bring different results in the way that they are cared for.

So, some hope is now developing that where in the past we have neglected the needs of our own world, that will end, and instead we'll develop a kinder and more caring attitude for the future.

Speaking Personally, apart from the information that I've received from both God and the Son of God, my work has brought me a role as correspondent with two powerful extraterrestrial spirit beings, and that has been fascinating.

But first, some years ago, I actually met a third being when I was working at a Mind Body Spirit Fayre in Glastonbury. In human form she was a tall transsexual and had a gentle voice. We talked a little about extraterrestrial life, and it was at that point that she allowed me to see her real identity. As I relaxed my eyes, I became aware of a very gentle and wise looking face that without doubt, came from another planet. I felt privileged that she trusted me enough to let me see her true self.

My second encounter was when I was living in Belper in the heart of England. I had been aware of a small being disappearing under the dresser in our living room. It was Jesus who then made me aware of Esquaygo's identity and explained that he was simply making his presence known to me.

I started to communicate with him, and I have many writings with information about his race, planet, and more. In fact, we corresponded for a long while before my husband, Mike and I moved to Spain.

Now, in my home in Andalusia, although I have communicated with Esquaygo, my work moved on largely to be with God and then in the summer of 2019, He told me that I also needed to talk to another very powerful extraterrestrial spirit being called Abuhindra. He said that he's here within the Earth plane to guide areas of healing that are beyond our human power but are essential for our sick planet. God told me that I would be working with both of them.

Superior Intelligence Or Not?

So, beings from other planets already communicate with us, but why?

As I write this, Turkey and Syria have just suffered a horrendously strong earthquake, and many countries are sending aid and rescuers to search for the living and the dead. We call it Humanitarian Aid.

Similarly, a group of beings from other areas of the Universe are here to help us save our planet, and we have never needed them more.

You won't see them walking down your local high street because they possess a far greater wisdom and skill and because of our potential to repel incomers, they can't be seen.

They're aware that they have developed much further than us on their spiritual and planetary paths; so, when they see us stumble and stagger through life with a lack of awareness and understanding, they feel a ***need*** to help us, because we must change but we don't yet realise how much.

I hope that once we are through this emergency on our own planet that we'll be wise and generous enough to return the favour. But first we must become aware that not only is Earth's energy at a low ebb, but it also affects the overall power of the Universe. So, although we may feel that the state of our planet is our business, the effect is, in fact, far reaching.

But to communicate with our extraterrestrial rescue team we must overcome the wariness held by our own race.

We may be an intelligent one but that doesn't, in any way, make us a ***superior*** one. We can't be while we dismiss the Power that governs this planet, and here I'm talking about God and not our world leaders. We lack the deep understanding that only that Deity can bring us. So, faith and trust are vital to our future. I'm not talking about religion although I don't exclude the power of those true to God's Purpose. Instead, I'm talking about a full relationship with God that guides and empowers us to heal our lives, and our planet and return to a positive and peaceful structure.

To start with, I have to say that it was both Esquaygo and Abuhindra who began our conversations. I was judged to be a receptive human, whereas I know that Esquaygo has tried to communicate before with other people and was rejected. Abuhindra also said he was surprised that I welcomed his communication.

As humans, we search for other planetary life, but what do we currently offer another race?

- An expectation that they possess a lower intelligence than ours.

- A lack of language communication? I have learned that at least some other races use telepathy rather more than speech, which is a far more accurate way of communicating.
- An immediate suspicion of their motives fired by our tendency to war with others.
- Our reluctance to change even when it means saving our planetary home.

Really, it doesn't bode well for a friendly coming together of races. The ego led leaders within a large part of our world already see themselves as being at the top of the power tree. So, can we trust them to welcome more intelligent races?

Certainly, while humanity remains on its negative and destructive path, our extraterrestrial neighbours will remain quietly in the background and pity us our blunders.

But the day must come soon when the world starts communicating with those beyond our perimeter.

Let's Consider The Overall Picture

First, the powers we see….

On Earth we accept, often grudgingly, the various lawmakers and human hierarchies that rule and guide our lives. Those include:
- Local councils and governments that are responsible for areas within life.
- State/ county control
- Regional control
- National government
- Heads of state and royalty
- Powerful international agencies that hold authority over some of the world's needs.

Then, there are the Powers we can't see….

Using the Name 'God' as a job description, consider the spirit-based hierarchy....

- God, the Spiritual Creator of life on Earth, has a base within the Spirit Realms, also known as the Heavenly Realms or Heaven and Hell.
- The Spirit Realms reach throughout the Universes.
- From that base, God has a support team of angels (varying levels and roles), spirit guides, and elementals that work with the angels, as well as our planet's valuable power.
- God has created and supported intelligent life on other planets within our Galaxy. Beyond God, there are more Spirit Beings of immense power, and they oversee the creation of life, as well as monitor the state and health of all planets within each Universe.
- In addition, there are more Gods (Creators and Supportive Spirit Beings) within our immense Galaxy, of which **our** God is just one.

Like a family tree, or a business authority model, the power in the Spirit Realms would be something like this;

The prime authority would be the Powers within the Galaxy and Universe they would be the *Overseeing Authority*

The next level of power and authority down from them will be those with the Creative and Restorative Powers and the area would include *God* (by whatever name you apply), and also *Abuhindra*, a spirit whose role is fully explained elsewhere.

The final level will be the Planetary Beings. This will include *Esquago* (from the planet Alubarium), the *Human Race*, and *Other Planetary Races*.

Again, I suggest here that we apply the word 'God' as a role rather than the Name of some remote figure on a throne.

I have been told that once a new planet has settled and is ready to support more than the most basic level of life, the overseeing Spirit Beings call on the appropriate God to fulfil the role of Creator and Support on it. It's at that point they decide what sort of life is needed to fulfil a new area of development.

In Earth's case there was a need for free will, and equal and opposing forces of good and evil. That was decided with the expectation that it would bring powerful learning of a different kind, which could at times be achieved through wrongdoing. The basis was that goodness always wins through with God's White Light at the helm.

There are also Spirit Beings, who carry the same level of power as God, but whose role is to answer the call when a planet has been seriously weakened and is losing the ability to support life or recover.

Abuhindra holds that role and has the responsibility of overseeing the healing and restoration of our planet, so that it may return to strength and once again provide a healthy base for humanity.

So, he now works within the Earth's plane and will continue to do so until the planet is healed, and life here resumes a safer course.

He came from the Bowoden race, and I asked if they lived a similar lifespan to humans. He said that they lived much longer than mankind but then reminded me that our Earthly life is only a tiny percentage of the main frame that we move on to in spirit, where our journey is immense.

Abuhindra The Leader

I also asked if he had been a leader, as his words brought a feeling of authority.

Abuhindra replied that he had led within his own country, long ago, and as a result, that had made him a different sort of being.

To illustrate the differences between our two races, he added that although they would flare up where some who presumed power fought for their place in society, it wasn't the same type of war as the uprisings that we see on Earth, and so overall it was more peaceful.

He continued by saying that some within the human race, have abused their people, and that irritated him, because his own race abhorred cruelty and despised lust.

He described the Bowoden way of life as one that welcomed growth, through their minds, and bodies, and by using techniques that established both a freedom and the goodness to serve God.

Their race's wish to bear children also united all types and classes, because the new generation was mixed and healed the divides, so they didn't develop factions within their society.

He compared it to ours within which he said he sees many factions, so advanced and divisive that the power struggle on Earth is clearly visible. The difficulty is therefore to achieve a structure that's fair and allows a powerful and peaceful growth.

At this point, Abuhindra poured out a great deal of information.

He said, 'I feel I must tell you a little more about the planet where I was a disciple of the worshipful God that many experience, and who has also brought a powerful current of life to the Earth planet.'

He said that when he was a young man, he bore little resemblance to the type of alien seen in so many of our films.

Adding, 'I was impatient to be of worth to my people, and I was resolute that I would bring good, and the power of virtue to all that I met.

We were a race of vastly differing types, as there are on Earth, and we had within us a need to bring good. It was profound, and we felt it deeply.

So, we applied ourselves to our planet, and developed a powerful and worthwhile structure to each area of work.

There was degradation in some areas, but we allowed a way of repair, and rebuilding; for the planet had undergone a great deal through a hazardous weather pattern.'

He added that they lived in small, but basic houses structured in a way that allowed a finer spread of light throughout, as that was precious. It was mainly dark when the bad weather struck, and it lasted many years before calm set a direction of good for them to take up a more suitable and worthwhile path.

He said, 'We are treasurers, workers, accountants and many work with the sciences, for they work with God's help, to maintain our alertness to bad weather or any other hazards which may cause harm to a planet.'

Discussing The Youth Within The Planetary Races

Abuhindra continued by saying, 'There are many disciplines within which we must live, to attain a power of diversity and growth. Yet I feel this is missing within the youth of some races that grow within our lands, whether they are of human race or some others within the planets that grow their aura in the Galaxy of Mia.'

He said that although they bring great value to the empowering part of life, there is a decline in some areas where the young, within themselves, look for more than the life they're allowed.

For this to be achieved there must be a growing understanding, therefore they're adjusting the criteria to fit the need.

Adding, 'So, when I see the human race applying itself in a more powerfully resentful way, I feel that there are areas within these, that do not fit our programme for growth, and adjustments must be made to allow more of it within.'

He said then, 'I feel now that there are both differences and similarities between the youth of our planets, and to forfeit the power that they bring is foolish. However, we must hone it to bring greater development, wisdom, and also to hold to goodness at all times.

I feel at one with saying this because I feel that our planetary experiences are similar in some ways, and the attitude that attains growth must bring colossal strength to the world, as they change the format of power for the future.'

Inhabited Planets Like Mars and Pluto

Abuhindra went on to say that some think that Mars is a habitable planet, and they're right, because it has a good and vibrant atmosphere and the humidity of a planet that's viable for fertile ground.

He said that many feel Pluto is too far to have the potential for habitation, but there's a force of people already inhabiting the planet, and it carries a basis of growth that's been in place for over a million years.

It's both a developed and worthwhile planet. Its air is clear but there's a basis of sulphur within the ground that's atmospherically disturbing to those who aren't from there. However, they're a race of good and worthwhile people, who enjoy their way of living in a similar way to Earth. It's simply that the air isn't as hospitable, and you must have some sort of filtration, if you're not from the planet itself, as breathing in the gases disturbs the throat.

He said that there are many on Earth, who feel disturbed by the fact of other life being out there, and yet it's not feasible to think there would only be life on this planet.

However, all inhabited planets throughout the universe are friendly, and it's not true to think that wars occur on them, or that they are the enemy. For that scenario, we must thank the writers and filmmakers.

Abuhindra said that there's a bias towards war on Earth, and if that can come to an end, there'll be a balance of friendship throughout the Universe and beyond.

He added that they hope that will happen, and that the world may move forward in full.

Lunar Power

One interesting piece of information that I received was about the Moon, and I can thank Jesus for this fascinating account.

He started on a cautionary note by saying that it wasn't a happy day for the Universe's interplanetary powers when mankind first landed on the Moon surface, because although it's a powerful planet it's also averse to disruption, and so the landing was seen as an unwise invasion.

Of course, there's been another more recent one in 2023, but I feel again that it will be seen as an unwise action.

The Moon supplies the wind and the formatting of the tides, and it also unites the fabric of planet Earth through its growth.

Its energy is within the skin of the Moon's surface, and in Jesus' words, 'It is a majestic and wondrous force' that allows it to combine a planetary strength with an abundance of land mass, and it's that mass that carries within it an enormous light that spreads across the Universe.'

He added that its versatile power affects the Universe as a whole and can also bring astounding effects.

He then went on to say something that may upset many historians and religious writers.

'At the time of my birth there was a partial eclipse of the Moon, and it equated with a starlit effect that defied the imagination. And yet they all believed it to be a star, and it wasn't. But so it is that man magnifies such mistakes and believes them willingly to be of truth and worth to the fabric of the story.'

He continued by saying that there's 'scientific proof' of many different things happening that cannot be, and so mankind's poor analysis brings doubt of such happenings, settling for partial proof, whereas it can all be told through the wisdom of God's Power.

He then moved on to the fact that the Moon provides light and energy at night, for those who need it, including many nocturnal creatures.

But just as that provides an answer that we can deduce on any clear night, there are some things that can surprise. For instance, lunar power does more than light the way, it also brings us as individuals a clarity of mind that can facilitate our growth.

Without the power of the Moon, we can experience discontent, and so it's important to the mind to have an avenue of clarity that can allow growth, and that's provided by the effective forces of the Moon.

It also glows brightly through winter which helps those with restless minds, and when needed, it combines with the Sun to restore the power and capability of the body; so, the result is a combined energy.

But the Moon also brings magical qualities to the world, and enchants it in many ways.

If there were no Moon, the human race would flounder. We would find that the creativity within us, was too little to bring about change. We would feel vastly reduced in power, and that would affect our ability to achieve results. So, it's a vital link to our life here on Earth, and, in our need to progress we don't help ourselves by diminishing the importance of either the Moon's power or the Sun's.

But it's so often emphasised in my writings that mankind believes that he's growing more powerful, and with that picture in his mind, he dismisses the effect of the various forces around him. Instead, he needs to accept a more realistic perspective of human intelligence as it rates alongside others.

Martians

We automatically assume that the human race was the first to inhabit Earth, but, in fact, another race came to this planet when it was basically a spent force, following the gales and weather changes that had happened over millions of years.

They came from another planet with a need to inhabit this one, but it was too humid for them, and they couldn't settle for long.

The Martian race is a hardy breed that has the ability to bring about change within their skin to suit their climate. But the power of the Sun was so enormous at that time, that it created immense humidity on Earth and didn't allow them to live a full life. However, they've now sustained a peaceful world within their own planet, Mars for many years.

They don't wish to war with anyone, and they don't expect mankind's intrusions onto their planet to create a problem, as long as the human race is aware that the life force is different, as is their lifestyle.

The area where most inhabit has no water, but that doesn't cause a problem because this is how the Martians live.

They are excited to think that we are a living Earth force ready to communicate, but if that were in a warlike way the people there would hate it. They need a gentle encounter because they are a loving and wise people, a far cry from the arrogant behaviour of some humans. So, it seems wise not to search for inhabitants or even evidence that they exist.

But it's accepted that the time is coming, when mankind will send a force of people to the planet, and they must not be menacing, no matter where they are.

Comparing Races And Purpose

I wanted to compare Abuhindra's race with my own, so I asked if there were male and female genders in the Bowoden people, and if they partnered in love.

He immediately replied that yes, they are able to reproduce between those who are attracted to each other, and the males have male glands whilst the female has a responding one; so, the way they show that love is through their bodies and their hearts, which again like the human heart, has a beat and together with the soul, will bring life.

He added, 'We are not dissimilar to the human race, only a little taller than some, but these are the variations that are found in many races,' and he continued by saying that they had a fabric within their society that delivers goodness and sound judgement, and that then allows a growth pattern for the development of their planet.

He said that when their planet was destroyed by massive explosions and its life was waning, some were able to salvage a power of seeing, so their future became multidimensional.

The Power To Strengthen Other Planets

Abuhindra went on to explain that this meant that they were given the power to serve other planets, and enfold their knowledge into a wider area of interest to those who knew nothing about the degradation of dying planets. They saved that knowledge in order to bring about changes that allowed a greater viability for those planets that would reject life, and that meant they could fulfil a need to serve the growth pattern within the solar system.

He said that there are many ways it can suffer degradation and upset, and it's necessary to resolve that problem from the aspect of those, who also wish to grow the power within their lives.

He then added, 'We resolve to be those beings who will bring a power of truth and wisdom to all life, and we endeavour to use that power fully in order to bring good to all that live within these terms.'

Focusing on our own planet, and inevitably its power within the solar system, he added, 'So we have to believe that when there is a planet that empowers the thoughts of those who bring both good and evil, that they can throw light on the magnitude of upset when ill takes over. There is a need for the planet Earth to survive, and it must bring a powerful result to our need for growth.

So, we respect the way this planet performs as a home for the human race, and we give our power to its need to survive, but we also look for the good to come from those who inhabit the Earth, and that is why we are here to help those, who inhabit a planet of lessening power.'

Surely those words illustrate the honesty of those who have committed to help us repair our planet. But at the same time they are stating quite candidly that the human race must now join the team, and play its part in reversing the world's decline. How can we argue with that?

Esquaygo's Description Of Alubarium

A few years ago, Esquaygo gave me a description of his planet, and it's interesting to see how much difference there is across our three planetary homes.

Esquaygo said that Alubarium is a place where much of the population live underground, and only venture into the light at times to come together and discuss an issue or bring light to the earth-like substance that covers their planet.

In 2016 God told me that many eloquent and powerful beings came from there.

Esquaygo explained that bringing light to the earth like substance on their planet means generating a vitality within the layer above the surface, so in order to achieve that, a party of them vitalise a certain area, and acting together, they link and pray to the same God as we do. Interestingly, He was the Deity on their planet long before life began here on Earth.

He described his race in this way, 'We're not like man in the way that he has fingers and thumbs to use, but instead we have a similar number of digits that allow us to reckon on an equation of five times four.'

He said that where mankind has a skull, and fingers that are almost talon like, his race has a smaller skull in proportion to their body size, and instead of talons or even tentacles, they have a small globular shaped hand with a series of digits that are used for counting, but in a different way to ours.

They use both the brain within their head and their hands; for there's a sensor in each hand that gradually assesses a touch allowing it to accumulate knowledge. The build and brainpower of an object or being is assessed in the stems of the fingers, and not by the eyes or other sensory structures.

Esquaygo said that he sees that as a development from where all brain power and wisdom is structured within the head, because it wastes parts of the brain which are not used fully. Whereas when it's placed within an area of the skin, where there's sensory placement, as in his own race, it can be of real value.

He continued to describe his race by saying that there's a need for air fracture within their heads in order to siphon out areas of gas, which are no use to the brain, but could inhibit its function; and so a visual capacitor is also at the base of the head, in order to bring to the fore brain function for the manipulation of their bodies.

He went on to say, 'You must understand that we're of high intelligence and can equate with the highest of God's understanding, so that factors about the earth can be brought into place by an easier method, than equating with each and every rational being within the planet, and then asking them to do what's needed to allow the planet a better and more enduring health.'

I also asked Esquaygo whether he had free will.

His reply was, 'No I have a will to bring forward the energies that are needed to govern life and build on it.'

He then referred to our own world's challenges by saying that he cherishes life and doesn't need the ups and downs of mankind's thinking, yet that is the construction organised for our race on Earth, where we must grow within the framework of someone with no limits, while at the same time keeping within the levels that can conform to a good power base.

For me, the frankness of these extraterrestrial spirit beings illustrates an openness to share knowledge, and with such superior intelligence, I would have thought that an alliance can only benefit our world as a whole.

Surely, we should now begin to acknowledge the friendship and help that others bring us.

But we must overcome that human default to immediate suspicion. It's an understanding that's fed and nourished by the inaccuracy of films, and books that constantly sow the seed of 'alien aggression'. Even the word 'alien' speaks of something that doesn't belong.

Suspicion can easily stem from ignorance, and it dams any flow of goodness. Yet if we communicate with God and the spirit plane who already do their best to bring us wisdom, we can learn so much more of our beginnings, our options, and welcome those friends from within the Universe who are working to help us. When we create alliances, we give ourselves space to grow in a positive way. Without it, the human race must remain isolated.

When we lack the crucial information, and intelligence that can allow us to better our lives and restore the planet, we lessen our power, and surely if we are to progress fully, we must focus on trust, and remove that huge barrier to our development, and more importantly, our survival.

The Diet And Humour On Alubarium

In 2011, Esquaygo expanded on his picture of life on their planet, adding that their food is a micro diet of small vegetables that grow in the light area within the ground, so they're able to harvest it at any time. Their need for light varies, as they can create it through a lithium-based substance found within the earth, and it's this that gives them light within the planet's crust and allows them to grow as individuals. He added that it's basic to their day within the ground.

He also said that it didn't mean they can't live above it. Their creative ability allows them to see the benefit of living underground, but they are also fully able to live on the surface.

He added that they have a sense of humour, together with a very creative mind, so they can see things as funny as we do here on Earth. In fact, he said that their humour can at times be an irritating form of slap stick comedy, adding then that in some ways they think like mankind and that there are many ways in which we could be friends. But he followed that by saying that it was too much to believe that they would be welcomed as a race apart from humans, and that very soon they would be viewed as an interfering mob. So, for the moment it seemed better to remain isolated, until the time when everything can be open, instead of concealed. Meanwhile each side must endure the secrecy.

Speaking Personally, Esquaygo made me laugh when he finished our chat by saying, 'Don't be astonished, my dear Frances, that we often share the same drink, and I enjoy a meal alongside you, as you are a very able cook, and I enjoy tasting the wisdom and power of human cooking, as there is much to be learned by it. It can bring an alert to the tongue, if there is a mite too much sugar, or other substance that's not quite to our taste; I enjoy feeling I can share with you in these ways.'

I must say that I found the time that Esquaygo spent with me both fascinating and illuminating.

Through him I learned that telepathy is used far more than the spoken word, and although I'm very much a beginner, I do feel it's a more accurate way of conversing. After all, it's a shorter process of transferring information from one person to another, so it must be better.

The Work Of Powers Within The Galaxy

A growing number of people question what is beyond our own planet, and space is experiencing more and more traffic as scientists explore the great beyond, but our world is only a tiny part of the Galaxy's potential. It has many 'Earth type' planets, and yes, there is life of some sort on many of them.

However, developed life exists on only a few, as it's necessary to bring a format for it to develop before it can be seen as habitable.

This is where the Gods, who conform to the role of our God, bring their skills to tailor a basis of life that will suit the races that need to develop.

These Programmers are a blessing because their strength and reasoning develops whole new directions of learning, so that the balance of growth on a planet can be versatile and vary according to the needs of the race that inhabits it.

Abuhindra admitted that in some ways, the spirit powers have failed in the past to explain the need for growth, and that they now realise that it's necessary, because of those who have limited knowledge, and simply don't understand what's needed of them.

He added that they must now bring fresh knowledge so that it instils a capability and a greater understanding. Because, as he said, 'The wisdom is there to be given, and it must develop the minds of all those, who feel they're alone on an inhabited planet, which bears life, and yet its place in the Galaxy, is beyond comprehension.'

His next words shine a true light on our part within a planetary community and why we must enrich it,

'We are, in fact, seasoned growers living our lives and developing a growth pattern that will bring a development of worth throughout the Galaxy, and it's now necessary to bring to the fore, a relationship which starts between us and our neighbours in each planetary formation within it.'

He said that we're all here to grow, and we have to develop from the early stages of mankind to a new and better version that will work. That way we will contribute to the formation of a pattern of growth throughout the Galaxy, for beyond us all lie many more. For us to succeed we must elevate mankind's thinking to a more prominent level, where he'll take action to stop the upset of the past, and play his part in the development of this Galaxy, and beyond the stars to new areas that need to grow.

I have had a growing realisation of the power of Abuhindra, so, ever inquisitive about my correspondent, I asked if he was one of the wise Planetary Beings that decide the future of planets, and the growth and health of them.

His reply was, 'There are many ways to describe my role here as the power behind changes that will happen over time, and it is fair to ask now if I am one of those who sit in council over the ways needed for this Earth and beyond, for I have the authority to do all that you say.

But beyond that, I also need to comply with the authority of those who delegate powerful Spirit Beings to oversee the pathway of others, where there is a problem. So, I was brought by those, who are of service to the needs of the whole Galaxy, to be of service to God's needs here on planet Earth.

As a delegate I was given choices of how best I could take forward the work, and it was given to me through the authority of those Higher Beings who foresee problems or upsets through the Galaxy. And they are the authority I bow to in my position as an ambassador for God, and all He does.'

At this point, I asked if it was God that decided that he and I should work together, because it was God who actually told me that I needed to work with this extraterrestrial Power.

Abuhindra's reply was clear. 'It was I who said to God that I felt there was an authority in what we could do; also, that I felt we could take forward a positive approach to the World's needs; and He felt it was worthwhile that we spoke, as it harmonised with the work you already do. I felt that too.'

And so that was how my work with Abuhindra began in 2019.

Those Who Leave Their Planets To Heal Earth

In every relationship whether spiritual, personal, or business, we should establish trust and Abuhindra wanted to bring a clear account of his background which would then shine some light on his work within the Earth plane. So, it was welcome when he continued by saying, 'I feel it would be good to tell you my origins and allow you to understand more of my intent here on Earth'.

He then said, 'It is often assumed that we, (the team that has come to Earth), are a diverse and unreliable asset to the benefit of whatever planet we choose to come to, because we are a varied race. But we are a whole. We have come from individual backgrounds in our own planets to act as a force for the benefit of the World we are in.

Many of us are from my planet of the Bowoden people, and that is because we bring a purposeful vibration (energy) and an instructive approach to the ground's value.

We can know in an instant if it is impenetrable at that point, or if it lacks water, or is a risky challenge for those who are to take the workload we give them.

For that, we have a brain force that is actually wiser than the best and most well-constructed human brains, and for that I am thankful, for it has served us well in our work throughout the planetary system.'

He then went on to describe others within the team, speaking of their special abilities and skills for working on and within our planetary home.

'Some of the smaller beings here are a gentle race from a planet in your own solar system, and that is called in our language Abwana, the land of solitude, for they stay close to the planet, but they are only in small areas of it, where it is fertile.

I feel now that the most agile are those of the Planet Cloose, which is close to the Earth in a different cycle. It can be seen with the naked eye when the Moon is high in the sky.

And they are most agile, and able to bring about changes that can reformat the Earth's energies when it is in a sense of shock from some explosion above ground.

They are vital to our search for answers in the need to construct a better level of forces for the Earth to react in a kinder and gentler way.

He said that they're blessed with those who are here to bring about a quality of goodness to the World, and that he would say that they are the best within this planetary system and can't be faulted.

He added that they're aware of the Earth's charms, but he believes it's more beautiful in the homeland of his people, as it has a beauty unhurt by mankind, as well as there being a more powerful and beneficial effect when there's no need to remove damaged substances, or endure constant war.

'He said, 'I feel now that we can bring a fire of enthusiasm to people's lives when they realise that we are not the grotesque beings they are taught to imagine, and that only through the acceptance of such powerful help, can they find a way to resolve many of the problems faced by the human race.'

Speaking Personally, I find it embarrassing that our friends from other planets see themselves represented in such an ignorant way on films and on television. Would we not be hurt and resentful if they judged us in the same way?

Instead, we should pause and appreciate that we have immensely skilled and caring beings here from their planets both to remedy the ills of Earth, and also to help the inhabitants. We may think, 'Well, okay then, it's job done', but in fact, Abuhindra explained to me about the loss of his own planet, and it suddenly helps you to understand the painful journey of losing the world you have always expected to be there.

When A Planet Is No Longer Habitable

He described it this way, 'There was a great explosion that devastated the whole surface of my home planet to some extent.

It was not an isolated one and the explosions carried through a momentous change in the formatting of the planet, so much in fact that it was impossible to live within its aura, and it was therefore a devastating experience, which cannot allow life of any kind for some time yet.'

He said that he feels that one day the planet will become more valuable, but that there will be many changes before it can be said to be suitable for life again. Meanwhile, it's stable.

The Power Of The Universe

Abuhindra confirms that when the power of the Universe comes together, it can be with force and genius, because it solves many problems, and it's alert to all needs, throughout the planets. He said that their objective is to see that they grow in strength and normality to retain the force within them, and that they develop in order to strengthen their aura. Of course, all living things possess an aura and a planet is no different.

He said that he and the other spirit beings that work with him are enthusiastic about their work, because they can see the variables in planets, and they're able to assess whether the force within is viable for a programme of fertility and growth.

Apparently, there are many variables that must be calibrated to ensure that the planet's health is within a ratio of growth that applies to plant health, and that the dynamics are there to apply a system of development to all those who inhabit it.

That's necessary because these powerful beings need to ensure that where viable, all planets can continue to grow for a million years, although some are known to be far less, and at the other end of the scale, there's one planet in the galaxy of Mia that has reached growth over the duration of one million, one hundred years, and some say that it's a powerful and habitable planet that's going on to bring even greater growth in its life term.

So, this is why Abuhindra is eager to see the future of Earth restored to a level, where we can all agree that this is a planet of huge value, and that it can again, in time, bring back the power and authority that once held it in high esteem. For it was before, and still is viable.

The human race needs to realise that this is a living planet, so it does feel rejection and upset from what we have done to it. To change that, we must be more vibrant and determined to bring growth, because at the moment Earth follows an unviable and upsetting direction because of its declining health.

Speaking Personally; About Other Planetary Beings, for some on Earth, there's still doubt about life on other planets, while others feel a tentative curiosity about the existence of extraterrestrial beings. But even when you allow for those who know there must be life beyond our planet, the human race has the tendency to distance themselves from 'the rest', and readily adopt the default attitude of 'us and them'.

But is it that clear cut? Are we really pure-bred humans?

It's fair to accept that we have each lived on Earth many times, and we may possibly close the book on our background because we feel it's complete. But the truth is that many of us have also lived on other planets too, and if your imagination doesn't stretch that far, well, it's time to start adjusting.

Although I have lived a number of lives on Earth, I'm still seen as a young soul here, but prior to that, I have lived on many other planets, so in all, I am seen as a mature soul.

I know that my husband, Mike has also lived on other planets, in fact God told me that we met on a planet called Fratoria. Mike has also lived here on Earth many times, and this may be his last life before moving on to other roles, but at times in the past he's divided his soul to live elsewhere in the Galaxy.

So, as you can see, depending on the level and direction of our learning, some of our lives may have been lived elsewhere, as well as experiencing those on Earth. So no pedigree Earthlings there then!

Personally, I find it a fascinating concept. But I think we must also consider that before we review our interplanetary passports, we owe it to Earth to heal the wounds that knowingly or unknowingly we have inflicted.

But just before we leave the subject of the planet Fratoria, let me fill in a little more information.

You may not see it because it's only visible to the naked eye at the height of summer, when the sun shines at a particular angle through the Universe and brings about a shaft of light that can be seen by man.

It was originally a wasteland but for one or two wisps of snowy grass when it formed 45 million years ago by human calculation, and the planet was apparently formed from another one's chippings.

It was rather grotesque in the beginning and then became aquatic before small areas of grassland started to develop and that led to flora and fauna. Once that happened, God was called to direct the energies of yet another planet. It was necessary to bring the quality of one land to another, and to bring the flow of life to each Earth through a lot of different ways. That happens because there are formats that can suit one planet, but not another far away. For instance, the life given to the soil may be one formula on Mars, but then on Earth it can be entirely different, and in the same way, the varying conditions can lead to different planetary races, and variations in the life they lead.

So, it's possible that you too have lived on other planets, but then we're just part of the same big family... A Universal Family.

Chapter 5: Earth's Beginnings

Earth's Beginnings
Including: The Early Formula; Mankind In Another Universe; Talking About Planet Earth; What We Learn Here From God.

The Early Formula
When it comes to the subject of Planet Earth's beginnings, science has a clear focus and doesn't compromise so, over a period of time assumptions have been made, and built on by those who prefer to see the human race as an independent power that's fully in control.

Among humankind's tendencies is a need to commit to extremes. Facts and opinions are stated by those who are not to be challenged, and so over time it's not questioned or tampered with, because the results are assumed to be completely correct. But no allowances are made for possible variations on those statements.

The birth of the planet is one of those examples that has dug a deep rift between the religions that claim that God created Earth, and the scientists who state clearly that proof exists of its beginning through the Big Bang, and so the existence of God has therefore, in their eyes, been disproved.

But there's partial truth on both sides.

When you combine elements of both arguments, you arrive at a far more revealing and fascinating picture because, although it's correct that God didn't create the planet, once it had settled to a stage, where it was seen as ready to host some level of life on a young Earth, the

Planetary Powers that oversee the state of the Universe, brought in God to begin the work of creation.

So again, there are glimpses of truth in both the science camp and religion's. But firmly held views in the God/ No God debate have been argued since time immemorial, and both sides are still entrenched; so, as the need for proof of this Deity has strengthened, more and more have moved to a stance of disbelief.

But we can no longer afford any lack of understanding, because as long as humanity continues to disbelieve such powers as God, both Earth and the human race weaken, and without immediate commitment to change, we'll not have the ability to save our planet, because we lack the power and wisdom that God can bring us.

So, we must now knock down the barriers of objection on both sides, and combine science's version and God's in order to find the actual truth about Earth's beginnings. In that way we allow space for belief to empower us.

After all, God doesn't need us to bow down before Him, He needs us to accept Him, and then get on with the practicalities of saving the planet.

The difference is that when we ask for the power to be given to us, we will be given the wisdom and strength to complete the job. That may sound hard to believe but it's actually as simple as that.

But before we explore that subject, let's first consider the fact that the human race was elsewhere before inhabiting this present planet we call Earth.

Mankind In Another Universe

For the information about this part of humankind's history, I have to be grateful to Esquaygo (meaning 'Little Person') the extraterrestrial from Alubarium, a planet situated at the other end of the Milky Way. He provided me with some of the information that I'm sharing here in this chapter, and I believe it provides answers to questions that we haven't even considered asking, and as a result, brings rather valuable depth to the beginnings of the human race.

He told me that although we're here now, there was some goodness left behind by mankind in some other areas of the Universe that they left. However, he added that he's not referring to this Universe but another, many millions of light miles away, and that it was there, where the human race first began.

Esquaygo said that humankind was found to be of value to the ground, as well as by the creatures of the planet.

He then added that it was a very different mankind and bore little similarity to this present world's.

In Esquaygo's words, 'intelligence ruled' and there was no lack of willingness when it came to bringing value and power to that Earth, so it made it worthwhile to the planet to expand the population and bring about good.

But despite that, that world still ended in a devastating cloud. It may seem drastic to us, but it happened so that another planet would form, and by destroying one it allowed the formation of a new one.

The purpose in creating this colossal new framework, was so that mankind would continue his past work, and so the seed was sown, and mankind went on to become the way he is today.

What the Powers hadn't anticipated was that the format of the human mind would continue to grow, and as that happened, his value as a spiritual being diminished.

This overt basis instead launched a new era of learning, but the quality that began to grow was rather more vile. It was an upsetting structure that was definitely not Earthly.

Whereas the mankind of the past had committed to kindness and been forthright and good, the human race as it is today, has a different commitment, focusing its growth on money and upset, with a basic structure of power; at the same time humankind considers itself to be of the greatest value to this world.

So, the spiritual purpose of life has diminished, and that isn't what the world or humanity needs. Meanwhile, there's no greater value to Earth than God, and no one else can commit as much love.

Esquaygo finished by saying that where humankind had been of value to the other planet very many Moons past, time has now shown that there's something other than God to distract him on this one.

Talking About Planet Earth

I rely on information from both God and Esquaygo to piece together a picture of the beginnings of Earth.

Newly formed, a planet isn't fit to inhabit, so, in the very beginning, soon after the Big Bang, Earth was both unstable and uninhabitable. There were no people, no animals, no plants, and at that point, no God.

But, as my various correspondents have previously mentioned, this Universe has more than one inhabited planet, and our God had already created life on others.

So once Earth had calmed enough to bring about some positive development, a committee of powerful Interplanetary Beings that keep constant watch over the state and health of each planet within this Universe, called on the services of the ethereal Being that we know as God, to bring life to Earth.

This is a situation that occurs in other Universes too, and, as I mentioned earlier, each has its own 'Gods' with the same Power to create, so you can see how, in simplistic terms the word 'God' is a role or job title, and I'm not being disrespectful by saying that it's simply explaining God's presence on this planet.

So once Earth had calmed, these powerful Beings assessed the situation, and decided that the time had arrived to call on God to bring a level of life.

Envisage if you can, that immediately after the Big Bang, there had been an immense blanket of ice which covered the planet, so it appeared completely frozen.

In a writing that I channelled from God in 2011, He, in fact, described it as a place of awe, and added that at that time it was sterile, and simply couldn't support vegetation.

But later on, once the planet had warmed a little, the ice caps became smaller, and it became more vibrant; so, where previously the ice had prohibited any growth, the stage had arrived where God could bring vitality to the Earth and with it, some hope for life.

That was the point of development where the wisdom and power that had been successfully used on some other planets came into play, and life on Earth began. It was apparently slow at the beginning, but as growth took place and sustained the planet, there became more value in the idea of bringing life to it.

First, the huge ice caps melted and that brought water to the ground.

Winds also vitalised the Earth and gradually they brought some stability. The air currents were slowly becoming gentler, and as they did, they became more able to correct the climate change to a point, where planet Earth could then sustain growth.

As it was, many valuable nutrients already existed within Earth, but a lot were now needed in order to bring the vitalisation that would give it life.

Esquaygo also gives us his version of the beginnings. As one of the planetary beings brought here by God, he was in a perfect position to describe more about the young planet.

He explained that as a newly formed world it was a dynamic piece of rock that bore no resemblance to what we have today. It gave off toxic gas, which waned after a millennium, and as the rock became richer it actually reached a point where plants would grow. And so, as the gas dispersed, it gradually became a more lucrative venture. Areas of the world were also becoming divided through huge blasts within Earth's atmosphere, and the gradual process of evolution began.

Esquaygo said that many of these spirits realised at that point, that if the power of water was to be found there, it would ultimately provide a source of life within the planet.

This brought a gigantic wave of activity within the Earth's crust that allowed icy globules to form, and as it did so it brought about liquid, and also molten lava.

A type of oil was produced through the friction of the huge rocks rubbing together, and that formed an oily substance that brought about earthquakes, because it gave off an energy that brought ultra-sonic waves to the many rocks, as well as the granite that formed up around them.

It was a period of dysfunction as the world evolved in stages, and until that was over, it would neither create nor support life. But the value was already there, and it was an interesting time, because there was so much movement felt within the Earth before it was ready for life to be given.

First great plates of rock rubbed together to format the Earth's surface, and then the oceans formed as vital areas filled with the liquid that was being displaced by the earth itself.

However, it took many centuries to form an even crust that was in any way able to bring about life, and this led to thoughts on whether it was the time to create life, or first of all, ensure a stable environment for the planet to survive.

That was essential because no Earth can support life if it isn't, at the same time, resilient to the power of evil. It carries the responsibility of all those who are either on it, or within it to bring value to the complete planet and not misuse it.

And so it was at that point that God was brought to the world in a need to sustain its growth. He had been of value to many Earths before this one and had brought life which in turn created a source of protection to the planets where He had sustained power.

But in the case of Planet Earth, the package of needs that was given to God, was one that would create something different, and that requirement came from the many Planetary Beings, who had overseen changes in their own spheres, and now were seeing a need to create a *new* world of light and power. And so, God was given the authority to move forward on a new scale, in order to create (in His words) the 'mightiness of Man'.

Now you may think that this was something that God did on His own, but a writing given to me by Esquaygo in 2011 actually confirmed that He did involve forces of other Planetary Beings in the work, as confirmed in his sentence, 'In the beginning of creation, we were there to bring the characteristics of man to the fore, through God's valuable intervention.'

With the current poor condition that our world is in, it's easy to heave the blame on the Creator, but then we're practiced at attaching fault to anyone but ourselves.

However, this is our work, it carries our signature and not God's. Through a lack of respect and love, we have conditioned the planet to a state of war, waste, and poisoning.

It carries a huge amount of negative energy and unforgiveness, and at no time was this in God's remit. His purpose was to create a world that would both nurture and release the wisdom and power that He brought to it, in order to satisfy the need for growth; and that would have been a positive energy for us to develop.

It was necessary to bring the vibrancy of Light and Joy to the world, and it was thought that the Universe could be valuable here by providing the ability and power to design such a creation.

Although many people still choose to believe that Earth was the first inhabited planet, God emphasises that He had already created many beings before that, just as He had been of value to many other Earths. He had done so both within the planet Mars, and also in other Galaxies beyond that of the world.

Maybe people assume that stance because they believe that not only are they destined to be *the* power within the Universe, but also that Earth is the intelligence base for many. But I feel that it's arrogant to see ourselves as so uniquely powerful. In fact, even God remarked, 'I feel at times it is Man who has created God's space within the world, and not Man who has been created *by* God.'

He even went on to say that although He's here to bring life and power to all who need it, He isn't valued as the incredible Power He is, and instead, there are those who have wrongly taken the power that has been given to them and added their own lust for authority over others.

But God adds that He sees little glimmers of light shining out down here, where those who bear this Deity's Word are given the right of truth, and take it forward, and to me that confirms the importance of us living in that way.

What We Learn Here From God

It's confirmed therefore, that planet Earth is in fact the result of a natural happening, and that in its 'raw state' it couldn't support life.

That certainly changed once it had calmed, and it was then that the Interplanetary Powers within this Universe evaluated the uninhabited planet and called on the experience of God to bring life to it. As well as giving it a viability that would benefit an inhabiting race, humans would then carry the responsibility of acting as curator to the animals, and nurturing a diverse plant kingdom. And so, just as we now benefit from the powerful energy of the living planet, we were also given the responsibility to maintain it.

However, such hopes and plans have been scuppered because the human race has developed a far more selfish power, which has now reached a point where even the planet is being treated as disposable and is therefore struggling to exist.

Chapter Six: Understanding the Planet's Needs

Including: Freewill With Good And Evil Forces; Rebuilding A Positive Formula; Interplanetary God; The Downward Slide Of Humanity; Speaking Personally; The Negative Forces Within Planet Earth; Symptoms Of Earth's Pain; The Need For Stability; The Imbalance Within The Planet; Describing More Symptoms Within A Sick Planet; Powers Beyond Ours; Speaking Personally; Comparing Planet Earth; The Ozone Layer; Creating Fertile Soil; Cloud Disturbance; Communication Between Outside Forces And Earth's Representatives; Speaking Personally; When God Calls For Help; Letting Past Destruction Prepare A Healthy Future; Saving The Earth From Dying; Scientists Play With Substances They Know Little About; The Danger Of Chemicals; Chemical Seepage Within The Earth; Human Obsession; Moving Forward In A Positive Way.

Freewill With Good And Evil Forces

I hope that as I piece together more information about Earth's place within the Universe, I can, at the same time, bring you some concept of the positivity and focus held by other planets' races.

In Chapter Five, **'Earth's Beginnings'**, I introduced you to the knowledge that long ago, mankind had inhabited another planet, where the success was in so many ways due to our race of people working together in a positive and powerful way.

On the 9th February 2023, I asked Abuhindra whether Humanity had the same free will and the same values of good and evil to work within during our existence on that other planet. He said, 'No,' and explained that it was a new concept to the Human Race when we came to our current Planet Earth, and added, 'It was a theory given to God to bring a future of exceptional worth, and it must now be at a point of adjustment, due to the calamitous reasoning of mankind to build on the authority of God rather than stay within His Principles.'

Sadly, we haven't repeated that previous success and instead, the logic of the human mind has been studied and wrongly identified as the main centre of humankind's intelligence and knowledge. So, it's become the focus for development.

Knowledge gleaned by the brain's logic has become king, and yet it's not the balanced understanding that we're meant to use, which includes such things as the natural skills and wisdom passed from parent to child, as well as the guidance of our conscience and instinct. The problem is that the soul isn't an organ that can be studied through a microscope, so even though it's within every cell of our human body, scientifically it's dismissed, and without knowledge of its presence we can't fully use our inner skills or fulfil our true journey of development.

The older balanced ways have been replaced, and are in danger of being lost completely, because they don't come with a certificate of verification.

They've had to make way for a more competitive form of life, where there's a need to focus on self-promotion and develop a more controlling power. Self-development, monetary reward, and status have become the new goals, but when you narrow your vision of life, it comes at a cost, because your heart's passion and your soul's guidance tend to go unheard; or if they are sensed, they're usually ignored as they don't conform to the required logic. So, when you do listen to them, and consider them, they may still get shouted down by your 'second thoughts', which come from the logical side of your brain.

The result can then be that you settle back in your not so comfortable comfort zone, climb back on that hamster wheel of predictability, and keep running. And yet another powerful and positive opportunity is missed.

In so many ways the true balance of human life is lost when logic is the sole driving force, and it's replaced by the glitz of a healthy bank balance, and a desperation to spend, and be seen spending, because it earns you social points and a misplaced pride in your prowess.

On the 1st June 2022, Abuhindra warned, 'For all those who think that the world is the way it needs to be, there is a shock coming. For the world is less able to care for itself, and it cannot foresee the troubles ahead.

He said that we must change the format of life if we are to bring solace and power back to Earth, and it won't be in a way that's enjoyed by those who sit back and feel no urge to help in the world. For they must take part in the work ahead and feel more grounded in the service of God if they are to survive in full.

I can confirm that although the inner reward felt by sharing and helping in the world may seem insignificant when it's weighed against the wow factor of a new car, that feel good factor lives on in your memory, and simply makes you want to do more. Life does have its reward when you step out of your comfort zone and develop that loving power.

In so many ways, human lives have become aggressive, and I don't mean just in the thuggish way seen too often on our streets, but also in our own ambitions and need for self-serving power.

We may have been taught or encouraged to follow that route, but ultimately that benefits no one because it doesn't provide a basis for true personal development, and it certainly doesn't help the world.

We don't have all the answers because we don't yet know all the questions to ask. It's as we devote ourselves to healing humanity and the planet, that we'll rediscover that special richness in our own lives, and the key to a safe and powerful future, both here and when our soul returns to our home in the Spirit Realms.

As we show our commitment to the healing of our world, we'll also be given the knowledge, power, and guidance to develop our skills still further, and spread the effect of our return to our true role as carers and curators of the world.

Rebuilding A Positive Formula

So how do we all return to a formula that creates goodness and positivity?

For me, it's gradually learning what sits well with you. When someone tells you something or it's in a book you read, or a programme you saw, it can feel so right that it awakens something within you.

It's almost like making your way through one of the world's many street markets, where the different stalls are shouting out about their services and tempting goods.

But when you make your way past the crowds, to the quiet man at the back, the quality shines out, and you know at once that he's the specialist that you need. For me that's God.

There's no glitz or glitter. That's for the ones at the front of the market. Everything on His stall is genuine and carries the maker's mark, and you know immediately that it's right, and you can trust it. You wonder why you haven't visited Him before, and then realise you were previously won over by the bling and loud voices at the front.

His message is more subtle and can be drowned out by those who shout so loudly to win your attention, and you wish suddenly that you'd taken more notice of everything that was on offer a long while ago. But then, it's never too late to change your Power supplier, is it?

Interplanetary God

As a race, we're possessive, so we may think of God as belonging solely to the Earth, but that's not the case.

In one of Abuhindra's writings in 2021, he spoke to me about the incredible Power that God possesses.

He began by describing Him as the Spirit that brings us together, and who allows the basis for advancement and growth in those worlds that He controls. And it's in that sentence that we have the first clue that our God has responsibilities in other planets too.

He said that this magnificent Energy has a great abundance of knowledge and understanding that's wrapped up within a Power of Infinite Love.

Expanding on our previous understanding of God, he added that He has mastered many worlds in the past and has brought forward great values and an abundance of growth, which then led, in his words 'to a need to establish a new fold of people who may overcome difficulties to produce a new way of learning through both good and evil'.

That sentence provides the clue to what God and the other Planetary Powers had planned, and that's why we have free will.

Humankind had already proved its power to develop good on that other planet, so there was no reason to believe that our people couldn't move on to even greater success on this new Earth.

But where the human race was expected to grow more powerful through overcoming difficulties, it has instead deviated, and over time, chosen to satisfy its hunger for a less powerful and more selfish formula of financial wealth and self-promotion.

The original blueprint given by God was one that made sense. After all, both areas of learning had the aim of bringing good, and at the same time bringing a greater understanding of evil and how to overcome it. It was thought that this programme of life could bring about a greater understanding of the harm done if it doesn't result in good.

To achieve this, the great Powers, who had committed to their own spheres in the past, came together to discuss this, solely to achieve growth, and then for the future of God's presence, providing a feeling of abundance that would radiate around the planet Earth.

The Downward Slide Of Humanity

The whole concept did begin in a full and moral way, but gradually through the centuries, mankind's attitude has instead brought upsetting violence, as well as an overwhelming insecurity for the world itself.

Abuhindra says that the dynamics within the world have changed so much that they are now being replaced by unrest, and an overpowering need for control by those who carry a lust for power.

Where before some adjustments could be made, powerful weaponry has grown to a point where it actually threatens the viability of the planet!

Let's just look at that sentence again... *'Powerful weaponry actually threatens the viability of the planet!'*

Prior to that message, in July 2014, God had spoken of the poor health of our planet.

He had warned that it's necessary to bring about a change that's so colossal it will be intimidating to anyone who sees it, and yet it must take place because *'the planet's viability has been damaged beyond anything that had been imagined!'*

Instead of Earth's status being elevated, it's been diminished through the world's need to govern with a violent authority.

Its value as a planet has been depressed, and the massive wave of chemicals used on it will bring a violent end to its authority if it's left alone to solve the issues, and in God's words,

'We cannot let this happen.'

He then went on to say that over the coming years there will be a change in the power of mankind, who's raped and plundered the Earth itself. That's where the authority of good will be given a vital opportunity to change the current path of destruction to a more temperate state of wellbeing.

He continued by saying that God's authority ***must*** be respected in this more powerful agenda, and that it will be imperative that work is done to save the planet from self-destruction.

He said that through the mayhem, mankind has severed all responsibility by taking precious oils and gases not only from the Earth's surface, but also deep down, where it forms a vital core for the planet itself.

He said that humans are running the Earth dry of all its resources, because the Sun's energy cannot replenish it in the necessary way, when it's not powerful enough to act in balance.

Humankind takes power for the world, in the form of electricity and gas, but Earth isn't now sound.

It's been drained of its resources for so long that it may destroy any hope of being revived if it's not protected by God, and not surprisingly, He fully intends to do this.

He said it needs to be stabilised so that it can grow and revitalise. This would ensure then that future generations would have a powerful protective formula.

Speaking Personally, the fact that our planet is dying is bad enough, but I'm ashamed that we're also inflicting this terrible situation on our children, and all generations following, because *we* have neglected to care for our beautiful Earth home. Instead, we've brought it to a point, where it struggles to defend itself through volcanic eruptions, earthquakes, flooding and more.

If we are to survive as a race, this precious planet must first be made safe. It's now that we must stage a comeback that brings true power of reason and value, and we must eradicate the upset of the past and draw in a new and viable love and hope for the future.

The dinosaurs were wiped out in a stroke, and for me those who build, supply, and choose to use such powerful and destructive weapons also belong to another age. They are harming the actual core of our planet, and with every powerful chemical we use, we're helping them.

The Negative Forces Within Planet Earth

Describing some of the pain within the planet, Abuhindra began by saying that when we see the flow of lava that comes from a volcano, we see the intensity of heat that has melted rock and we may understand that an eruption has resulted in the fire that's forcing it upwards. Where that may be an amazing happening for some, for others it can be life taking or, at the very least, life changing.

But what we don't understand is for that to happen there has to be a greater power, which then instigates that force. And that has come as a result of the Earth needing to evict upsetting energies within it, almost like a stomach does when it holds something which isn't good.

When that force erupts, it then allows a free flow of the destructive energies that must be evicted, and that will happen whenever it needs to.

But Abuhindra went on to say, '*We are afraid now that the forces within the Earth are too great*, and they are upsetting the equilibrium within the great planet. So, in the same way as I described, these forces will continue to affect for all time, if we don't soon bring some calm within the world.'

He explained that humankind's potent strength on the surface, can affect the ones within, if they are great enough, and the weaponry within each army is so great it will affect the world, and even deep within the planet.

That's because it upsets the balance, so the need for calm is evident, for imbalance can affect the whole planet in a second.

He said, 'What we believe is that within the source of the Earth there is a dynamism that is very powerful, but it's restrained from movement due to the heaviness forced upon it.'

He then made a very frightening statement.

'*It's that load that brings stability, and if it's moved through mankind's interventions, it will bring a dynamic force that's greater than the constraint, and it will unbalance the Earth so that it's no longer stable.*'

Weaponry is seen as the major cause of this developing weakness.

Symptoms Of Earth's Pain

Within this chapter you'll see that there are many ways in which Earth can suffer. Meanwhile we, the inhabitants, continue to ignore the signs that pour out of it.

The many volcanic eruptions mean that there have been a series of upsets within the Earth's crust that bring it pain, and when the planet erupts it's at a point of erasing the forces that interrupt the smooth flow of lava within the core.

It's essential that there's less cause for this to happen, and that means also easing back on the mining and upsetting explorative activities within the Earth that can upset the flow of a genial energy.

The Need For Stability

Throughout the Earth there is a need to bring stability. But first we need to better understand its power, because it has an energy which, when combined with the force of man, can have a beneficial effect on the world.

But when there's a constant need for the human race to use explosives or interrupt the flow of good energy through the use of corrosive and dangerous chemicals, it's not compatible with a powerful future.

So, if humanity wants to bring about a powerful and substantial future for all involved, it's essential that it revises its plans.

The Imbalance Within The Planet

Over several weeks and months, Abuhindra enlarged on the dangers that we face, due to the problems we're causing.

He began by saying that there are many ways in which the world falters, and so, it's bringing an imbalance rather than stability to the planet. He said he could bring solutions, and a better way of thinking to the human race, adding that he was ready to understand more ways of helping the Earth to suffer less and bring that strength to a higher level, where the planet will then become more capable.

He said he was also ready to use a way of inducing balance that would benefit everyone, so that the planet can then return to a lasting state of equilibrium rather than the present imbalance that's so disturbing. He said that the world needed to 'flow' better, so that it would then prompt Earth to take a more secure and vibrant course of growth.

Describing More Symptoms Within A Sick Planet

Abuhindra continued by saying that when the interplanetary team reach certain cavernous parts within Earth, there's a gaseous substance that gives off a caustic smell, and makes them nauseous; but he added that it's happening because that area of the planet is upset through imbalances in its system.

He said that when it was young it was able to deal with the levels of upset that were brought on it by certain non-conforming beasts and mankind, and so it was of little consequence to Earth. But the current problem started once the artillery and other areas of weaponry became more powerful, and ever since, there's been a growing unease within the Earth. Now it's reached a point where the planet finds itself embattled on all sides by the dumping of chemicals, and constant wars.

He moved on to speak of the dangers of chemical weapons, and that was supported by a writing from God in April 2018, where He also spoke of the need for them to no longer be a threat to the world.

So, whether viewed independently or as part of the whole, this is a real worry because the Earth is now combatting a sickness within it. Where it was once a vibrant planet, it no longer feels it, and that's due to so many substances harming it. In fact, it's growing old inside, despite still being a young planet. But, in truth it's enduring far more than it can deal with, and within its heart it knows no peace.

This is where we must emphasise that ***this is a living planet!*** It's not an inert object that we inhabit.

If any of us suffer constant hurt, we eventually reach a point where we need to defend ourselves. In simple terms we've been hurting the world as a whole for too long, and we have shown it no sensitivity or reverence. But now it's abundantly clear that it's not happy, and each 'natural disaster' endorses that.

Abuhindra went on to say that by bringing in forces from other planets there has been some respite, but that's not enough, and we have to continue the repair with forces that are then able to reverse the degradation of the Earth's soul, and lift it to a level where once again, it can accept a more powerful force of good.

It was then that he made a statement that humanity cannot afford to ignore.

'We are at a critical stage of the Earth's deterioration, and we need to see within the coming 600 years, a better way of valuing and renovating this planet, for it to be recoverable in full.'

The clock is ticking. Can we afford to ignore this warning, because the consequences are unimaginable if humanity doesn't rise to the challenge?

What we're encountering now in natural disasters is nothing compared to the hell on Earth that future generations will experience if we do nothing, and that will continue until eventually the planet either returns to an uninhabitable state or it's destroyed completely. Where will the human race be then?

Surely no one with a conscience can watch our world deteriorate, without resolving some of the issues that we're talking about here.

With that thought in our minds, let's understand some of the power around us.

Powers Beyond Ours

When he began to talk about the ways in which changes can be made throughout the Universe, Abuhindra started by saying that there are ways of doing enchanted things.

He must have seen the look of fascination on my face because he went on to say, 'There are ways of opening up the Universe's Power to bring about change that's crucial to our planetary system; and there are those who decide when that may be done, in order to be of advantage to a planet's formation.

At a stroke we can change this or that about a planet's atmosphere, so that it can avoid a meltdown, or an upsetting state of events that lead to its destruction.'

That level of true power seems incredible to my human brain, so I was grateful when he went on to describe a tool that we as humans have available to us. A tool that provides, in his words, 'one way in which a planet can be helped to heal its wounds'. It's available to us all. Prayer.

Through prayer and perseverance, the way a planet's core is behaving can be changed to hold back eruptions, and instead allow a recharging of the core to take place.

He continued by saying, 'Many of us are skilled in the need to hold back an eruption should it be required, but we can also feel the Earth calm down when there is prayer there to help it.'

Speaking Personally, I'm sure that for many this may seem too simplistic to offer a reasonable explanation, but although as human beings we see prayers simply as words, when we speak those words they become an energy, and when that is a prayer, the words become positive energies and en masse that can be a powerful force.

So, in this situation a healing energy is formed that can help balance the core and allow a calm to fall over the whole of it.

With that, he gave me the prayer, which I shared with the lovely members of our Love Worldwide Prayer Group.

So join me in saying this daily, and let's add our strength and love to heal the planet. I have listed all relevant prayers in Section 3 and that's where you'll find the **Prayer for Healing Planet Earth**. The more people who use it, the more powerful will be the result.

Comparing Planet Earth

If you have never really been interested in our planet except in the way that it offers you an opportunity for existence, I hope that the information collectively within these chapters helps you to understand that when it was healthy, the Earth had immense power, and it used that to empower us in some ways. So, it's been, and still is an important and integral part of our lives, but its current strength has been greatly depleted.

In the past, we haven't sufficiently included Earth in our life equation. It's been there, and there's been an assumption that no matter what happens, it always will be. How wrong can you be?

The question is, 'How does a weakened planet compare with others within the Universe'?

Abuhindra put it like this....

'When the planet suffers, so does the world as a whole, and it impacts not only in the suffering of the people, but also in the way that the Earth itself can diversify its energies.

It can shine out as a planet, but not fully, and that brings an aura that's lacking within the sky and beyond.'

He explained that all planets have an aura that can affect the balance within the Universe, and that enhances the growth within them all, because it fuels them in a way whereby they provide better value for those who inhabit them, and for all the properties within that planet to shine out, and bring good energies not only for their own benefit, but also that of the Universe.

But he added, 'We must now describe Earth as a sick planet, and it shines as a glimmer of what it once was'.

He reiterated that it's imperative that we bring changes. He said that we must alert the world to the fact that Earth's survival is in our hands, and we need to allow growth again.

You may question the way I say,' allow growth', but in truth, we can create barriers.

There can be those who simply think, 'Well, I'm not stopping it from growing', and leave it at that. There are also people who exercise their free will and say, 'I'm not doing that.' And in both those cases, by not acting they are excluding themselves from the act of healing, which then lessens the overall level of development in the world.

They deny themselves the foresight to accept what's essential to life, and that, with their cooperation, they too would enjoy the value and growth it can bring to everyone.

I hope I have your attention, because this information is brought by Abuhindra, who has a level of power equal to God, but in a different specialist area.

This amazing spirit being who's working with others within our planet, explained to me that just as God creates and empowers planets and the races that inhabit them, he, Abuhindra has the power to bring a planet back from an extremely weakened state to a point where its power is renewed, and it can then continue to heal itself and support the lives that are so reliant on it.

But he added that he can't do that alone, and just as he has a team working with him, we too must play our part, and that involves a lot of changes, which I include in this chapter.

Of course, with the very limited knowledge we already possess about the workings of this planet, I feel it's imperative that we now learn more from those who do know.

In October 2019 Abuhindra said that he was ready to believe that our future was blessed and said he hoped that there will be a time soon, where a belief develops between other planets and ours so that we can collaborate, but he didn't see that happening for some time.

However, he did add that the fact he and I were communicating must bring hope of a kind. I certainly agree that we, the human race must, at some point soon, ditch our myopic views, and recognise that friendly life really does exist outside our planetary home.

As Abuhindra points out, it's information that can bring a greater vibrancy and power to, what has now become, a depleted planet, and it can work in many ways to adjust the energies within its core.

He began by saying that there are many who believe that the Earth's core is a magnet, which is fluid based, and that's partially correct.

The difference is in its ability to boost its magnetic aura, which is held in place by the gravitational pull of the Earth; and that allows a force to exist that is therapeutic, and worthwhile to the Earth itself.

However, at the very time when it needs a kind and fulfilling aura of strength, it has instead a broken and less vigorous one; so, it can't heal all the necessary points within the Earth that will then allow it a robust quality.

The energy field or aura surrounds all living things, but sadly, we haven't viewed the planet as the living being that it truly is, and if we fail to respect and nurture life, we cannot fully appreciate or heal the world as a whole. So, step by step we must work to bring back the love, care, and respect that every area of life deserves, because without that we seriously affect the delicate balance that's necessary for it to continue in a positive way.

My spirit friend then expanded in this way about the elements that are bringing such pain to our planet.

He talked about the great and destructive weals of pain on the Earth's surface and continued by saying that they are there because our race is constantly at war; and that simply cannot continue if the planet is to fulfil its role as a secure and powerful home for the world itself.

He said that Earth's affected by both mankind's need for war, and also the powerful chemicals that are so intrusive to the atmosphere, so the surface can't transmit its fiery authority to the core, and fully repair the fabric of the Earth.

He said that the core needs to be regulated, which means cooling it in a way that will allow it to absorb healing.

Interestingly, he explained that it's a vibrancy they can transmit, but it's beyond the ability of humans.

He said that they hold a power that can successfully reduce the Earth's core to a far more empowering level, and that they achieve it through their ability to transfer their healing thoughts, while holding within them an energy that can level out the strength within the core.

He described it as a type of mind work, which allows the core to be seen in the minds of their many workers, and they reduce with a combined thought, the level of furnace within the core.

This eases the pain for the Earth, but it still can't progress as a planetary power, until mankind also finds a way to reduce the negative forces that are upsetting both the world, and the planet. The structure is still too frail.

He spoke of many other planetary beings that are here within Earth, working to prevent the degradation of the planet. They are at the base of the Earth's work and use old mines and cavernous areas as their homes, but they can only be seen by those who are friends, and, as he added, that cannot extend to the human race at this time as it would bode disaster.

The Ozone Layer

Abuhindra then turned the focus to the ozone layer, saying that if we are to cure the Earth of its ills, and allow it to develop the force within it, we must also focus on the winds that surround the planet at all times and calm the forces that are irritating both the Earth itself, as well as those who live on it.

He said that the valuable layers within the atmosphere are disturbed by us burning so much fossil fuel. Together with that there are the chemicals that we apply to the ground because they can also invade the space above and promote a problematic mixture of substances.

All these damage the ozone layer, and although much is said about it, there's little being done to eradicate the source of the problem.

These are yet more areas that we must soon attend to, if we are to prevent the fabric of the Earth being harmed even more.'

He ended by saying, 'We must protect the Earth'.

Just as Abuhindra now highlights the problems with the ozone layer, in 2011 Esquaygo had also spoken about the effect that mankind has had on the clouds, wind and water.

Creating Fertile Soil

First, he spoke about the many areas of the world where the ground needs energising with water in order to make it workable but said that it was possible to create more fertile ground without a heavy reliance on it. He said that there's clearly a need for more than water where there's a lack of phosphorus and iron, and yet, in some areas of the world if they act in the right way, they can survive and raise crops without it.

He added that it's the situation, where the human race needs to use prayer, and that by praying for the information to be given, they will find out how to lift the value of the ground to a point where it's a good quality of soil without the need for water; going on to say that if an area of ground is phosphorus rich, it can provide a reasonable level of growth even if it's given only half the water that would usually be used, and he added that if allowed, this will bring good crops.

Esquaygo said that to achieve this the soil needs to prosper from the rich mineral content, and that if we leave those natural minerals rather than removing them by working the soil, and then replacing them with chemical fertilisers, we'll see a level of fruit and vegetable growth far higher than before.

Also, if we treat the ground gently as we nurture the Earth's power, we should also realise that we are, at the same time, empowering ourselves with a new way of thinking.

Cloud Disturbance

He then moved on to the subject of clouds, saying that there is a need to improve our understanding of clouds if we are to help the world.

He said that at times parts of the world inexplicably suffer drought, and that it's not due to the wind but instead it can be caused by the way aircraft disturb cloud formations.

He explained that the power of wind is dislodged by an aircraft, and with the void it creates, it can provide a basis that prompts storms, high winds, or hurricanes to follow. He said that he understood that there's a need for some air travel, which will cause disruptive forces, but he then said that the exhalation of an aircraft's exhaust can vibrate through the clouds causing a powerful effect that, in some ways, can be stronger than a hurricane, and also cause vibrations throughout the world.

He finished by saying that the problem lies in the number of aircraft. It's not just a few. It's many and because of that it can be the catalyst for a furore of weather changes.

Communication Between Outside Forces And Earth's Representatives

Abuhindra explained that we need to understand that those who keep vigil for the Earth are beyond the intelligence of our human brain. They've gained knowledge that can bring them the Power of God throughout their need to deliver protection, and he emphasised that it's *solely protection,* because they obey the code of God's Law.

He added that he believes that if you brought such information to a human mind, it couldn't accept the authority with which it must be handled, and therefore it could have a powerful and unbalancing effect on the world as a whole.

But he added, 'Who knows? When the world is more able to accept such knowledge, it will hold such balance as is necessary to remove the upset of the past, and dedicate power and truth to the future needs of the planet, and those inhabiting it.'

He did go on to say that there are many decisions that must now be made for the formula of that future to achieve the accuracy and power needed by both the people who handle it, and the world itself; and he hoped that we could soon advocate a need to bring a more superior force to mankind than he holds at this time.

He then added in a very serious tone, *'For never before has the human race been at such a low ebb, and as we greet the day, we're anxious; for so many are at risk at the hands of those whose authority has been blatantly abused.'*

He said that such leaders are abhorrent in the cause for peace, and caring, and there must be a forthrightness concerning the abuse of power so that there's a more satisfactory result, and those in need are able to live fully and know the goodness available to them.

Through Abuhindra's words we can see that although the leaders within our planet may view themselves as not being answerable to a higher power, those beyond Earth have seen and been seriously concerned about some of the controlling authorities within our world. It's evident to them that some don't bring good to the planet or its people, but instead they manipulate it to satisfy their own needs.

He continued by saying that He felt that massive changes must happen first, for the world to act in such a way that both sides could communicate together. He felt that there was a powerful resistance to change within the world, because it holds the attitude that all is well. But he spoke positively when he said that he felt now that they would take forward a more compatible liaison with those of the human race who listen to their words, and act upon them.

He said he felt within a need to justify the moves they make to bring a vibrancy and power back to the Earth's core; but added that it's a necessary change, because it couldn't fulfil a purpose allowing a planet of great value to struggle to grow and be devoured by the restlessness of its occupants.

Abuhindra added that he's bringing valuable information to those who need to learn a more powerful, and constructive way forward, and understand more of Earth's power. Yet he said he feels out of place with these people as they don't accept the need for help, and they're out of sync with those who wish to save the planet. So how are they to be helped?

He then said, 'We have the authority to overturn wishes of the human race in their need to destroy a planet of goodness, but we hold no wish to do this, and the very thought of such a move makes me feel like an invader, and not the friend I wish to be.

So, I say now that I am ready to pursue all forms of communication to bring this planet's force to a higher value and pursue the need to continue in a powerful and friendly form to act with the human race to protect the Earth's values. Let it be soon that we can do that with the power that generates good, and make that happen'.

Surely the fact that we have an interplanetary force within areas of our world must make us realise how closely the powers within the Universe monitor the health of each planet, and ultimately, we must learn from this situation, and join the fight to return Earth to full health. Maybe then history will teach new generations how close the human race came to destroying both itself and the planet, so it never happens again.

Speaking Personally, I have always seen it as a privilege to be able to communicate with someone from another planet, so it was a surprise to me when Abuhindra said this early on in our communications.

'I feel jubilant that we have come this far in such a short time. For it was with apprehension I began to talk, as I have seen the evasive manner in which many (humans) take forward their lives and show little inclination towards a new and powerful ally.'

I was amazed, and to be truthful, ashamed that a friendly being who originates from another planet, cannot feel welcome, especially when they're here to use their superior skills to help us.

I do despair at those who have in the past, and still do create a fear of communication with interplanetary beings. Those with little or no knowledge jump in with their preformed opinions and ideas, and immediately create a barrier between us and our natural neighbours here in the Universe. Even the majority of science fiction, whether it's in films or written works, builds a hate relationship.

To me, it seems arrogant to view humans as a superior race, and I think that in taking that path, the world is trying to project a false hierarchy of intelligence, and for as long as we fail to connect fully with God's Power, we won't have anything against which to measure our authority and knowledge. Meanwhile if we want to be a full and active part of this Universal community, we must first join as a junior member, because we have a lot of learning to catch up on.

One vital reason for this is that other planetary beings already accept and work with God's Power as a basis of their lives, and they follow His Code. The result is that their lives focus on developing goodness and growth, and that has lifted them to a higher level of intelligence and understanding than we possess.

The human race, on the other hand, has developed a more blinkered approach by developing a harsher competitiveness and a self-promoting attitude, with material and financial goals that may measure a person's worth here on Earth but are irrelevant to our overall journey in spirit.

Our vision is for the development of logic without a need for the inspirational value that the soul can bring. The balance has therefore been lost because our link with God has been largely dismissed as insignificant or even fictional.

If we are to assume our true power, we must stop accepting the gaudy versions of it and focus on the real thing, and the sooner that we accept our limitations, the earlier it will be that we can openly communicate with those interplanetary beings who come here as friends.

Meanwhile, I'm grateful to Abuhindra who handles this situation in such a sensitive way.

Continuing Our Conversation…

I have left this next part in Abuhindra's own words as I feel they're clear for us all to understand.

When he communicated back in October 2019, he said, 'I am ready now to give more information in order to help our journey forward together. I hope for a long and happy understanding that is of great value to us all, as we take forward the needs of the Earth.

I am here to guide and direct our work within the Earth, as I have the attitude of a leader born with the need to serve.

I direct our thoughts to that area of work that will take us forward, and that allows a new and powerful force to be given in the Name of God, for this Power directs us to the needs of all planets within this Solar System, as well as others beyond it.

I feel now that we generally fulfil a path according to the needs of God, and that can bring a viable way forward for those who inhabit a planet to be able to achieve their needs.

There are always hazards of course and that may include the danger involved in the work itself; so, we take safety as a priority.

For like the human race we are easily hurt and wounded, so the needs of each must include a force of healing that can remedy an accident or indeed a calamity of the brain; for we have to endure much stress within our work too.'

When God Calls For Help

Some sentences just grab your attention.

'Let me be frank with you' was one, and Abuhindra then continued by saying this.

'We are here at God's Will, and to bring solace and a better expectation to a planet that suffers. Let it be (understood) that we are a conciliatory race formed of those who bring no harm, but only help, and the wisdom to allow a way forward for all those who are of great value to the Earth.'

I found it interesting that he was able to describe their approach to the work, giving the opportunity for others to take part later, and allowing this work the complete knowledge that's necessary to our path together for healing planet Earth.

He added that he believed that the awakening of (human) minds was not far off, and that he found it pleasing to think that it would clear any apprehension and upset for those, who fear beings from another planet, and it would instead replace it with greetings and a buoyant friendship.

He said that he recognises that their life together varies in attitude to the needs of the Earth, but that he feels that at the moment there is no incentive to strongly change the format of the past. But that once facts are known fully, there will be an energised decision throughout the planet that says,' we must do what is told to us if we are to save the world, and we must do it now'.

He also said that he can see a power developing that will bring back a vibrancy to the Earth and an understanding given to every man, woman, and child, that there must be ***no more warfare***, but instead a power of restoration, and that such goodness will then endow wisdom and strength for everyone who's involved.

Reassuringly, he finished by saying, 'I do this in the knowing of all that's good'.

Letting Past Destruction Prepare A Healthy Future

This powerful spirit friend has said that we're at a point where the world will realise that inaction will cost lives, and that we must cherish what is good, and know that the authority this will bring will allow far more vitality, if the human race then permits itself to progress towards peace.

He remarked that everyone seemed inclined towards aggression rather than peace, so he felt that if this can be curbed, there would be a more viable and powerful route forward and the power is there for those who decide to take this course.

He then added that when we only speak of war, pain, and the degradation of people, we can only see upset, and a world that's unruly and can't survive its own actions.

It's because of this that my work with Abuhindra began and, as he pointed out, the past cannot bring a more powerful world, so instead such destructive actions, and the upset endured by the planet would speak of a devastating future, rather than bring goodness and empowerment for the human race.

In fact, the hate by which it's bound can't bring a powerful future for the Earth, and it certainly won't bring joy to the people if the planet degrades yet further and brings even more hazards through climatic forces and upsets.

Again, this sentence rings alarm bells in my head, *'If we cannot unite the world on a path of reconstructive worth within the next 600 years, such little change will simply allow the Earth to fire more and more attacks on itself.'*

Yet the way it's treated leads only to fury, and an angry Earth breeds its own form of hate. That force is a destructive power beyond anything that we humans have encountered, so mankind's power will mean nothing to the planet, and it will become a landscape of destruction that's not habitable to any living being.

In June 2021, Abuhindra said that many understand that the weather rules, and this is the power the Earth has to retaliate.

It's the force that brings great vitality to the Earth, and when the power diminishes it yields uncontrollable forces that then bring dire consequences to all those that are vulnerable. So, we must realise the power of climate change, and the inferno that will follow when the Earth dies.

Saving The Earth From Dying

On the 11 February 2020, Abuhindra explained that the Earth is balanced so that the Sun is beneficial to the whole planet. But then he added that if we fail to bring changes within 600 years, the Sun may draw close, and our planet explode because of the poor treatment that Humankind has inflicted on it.

He then repeated the same message again that while they wait to see what the world will say to a new and more powerful direction, the Earth still needs help to ensure that it doesn't weaken, for without it, this simply isn't viable.

He said that the planet has been of strength to the world's needs for many centuries, and this has been good, because it's brought a balance and purpose to the whole of it.

Following on from that, he added that he feels now that if the world is equipped with a sense of value and purpose, it can then also understand the desperation in our interplanetary friends' words as they say, 'We need your help to save the Earth from dying'. And that will bring a powerful and positive response that will allow the world to know that they too are passionately involved in the needs of the Earth and its people.

And hopefully, that will enable them to move forward in full and bring that vitality and joyful purpose to the Earth, that can be used to instruct and advise all future generations, so that the help will also be there for them, and they can again grow in the stability and power of God's Love.

Scientists Play With Substances They Know Little About

And so, we must focus on yet another part of humankind's adapted formula, as we prepare for the beginning of a new and healing era.

Abuhindra broached the subject by saying that there are many things that interfere with the gravitational pull in Earth's atmosphere, and that this is brought about by many radioactive substances that lie hidden from the eye, but although unseen, they have been affecting the Earth.

He said that for a radioactive substance to work, it must radiate a field of energy great enough to encompass the Earth's atmosphere and control the power within it.

He moved on by saying, 'I can see that although scientists have taught the world trust, they are playing with a substance they know very little about. Yes, it has been a powerful energy that gives off heat and value in many ways. Yet it has an uncontrollable quality that cannot be tamed or reversed, and I feel now that it can only cause more deaths as it's used further in the world.

For the main nucleus of all explosions is hydrogen and it can give off a powerful odour, which is able to be detected, but when mixed with other substances, it gives off a power of destruction and upset, for it will combine easily and affect the nerves of all those within its reach, as all nerve gases do.'

He added without reserve, 'It cannot be that within the world there is a dark substance that threatens the lives of all those who live here. For that has radiation properties within its mixes that can eradicate life.'

He added that very little is known of the nuclear effect, and so it's important to say that the world can no longer rely on the substances that they can't understand, and it must now change to a safer way forward that can bring value and purpose back to people.

He pointed out that there are many affected through cancers and upsetting diseases and that leads them to believe that only a small part of the truth is yet available to everyone, and to know more we must all wait, and anticipate the widely used powerful substances that cause evil to appear in people's lives here on Earth.'

The Danger Of Chemicals

He continued by saying, *'I feel now possessed by a need to tell all mankind, and womankind of course, that there is a need to change some of their values quickly, for they will bring an end to civilisation ultimately through their erratic and uncontrolled ways.'*

He added that they bring a powerful area of chemicals to everyday life, and yet it's a toxic waste that does nothing to enhance the future of wildlife, or the ocean's mammals and fish. The waste products are seeping through all areas of the ground and then into the water, giving it both a potent smell and an obstructive force for the area of ground or water that it reaches.

He said that it's powers like this that allow a chemical build up within every person in that vicinity, and that he felt empowered to say that, through these mainly chemical forces there are build ups that will bring mayhem to a person's breathing. This is because it affects the lungs and diaphragm area where the power of the muscle slackens, and that then brings a shortage of breath, and a need to cough more.

Chemical Seepage Within The Earth

In February 2020 Abuhindra spoke over two days about the effects of chemicals both on and within the planet.

He started by saying that the Earth acts in a way that we would if someone threw chemicals at us, and that it's a living thing and naturally reacts when we abuse it.

He said that although farmers and scientists believe chemicals are essential to bringing good to the land, they are actually an irritant, and so as a result the earth cannot balance properly.

There is also an amount of those chemicals that pass into the hearts and lungs of those eating the produce grown on that land, and that therefore affects the end consumer whether that's people or animals.

Moving deeper into the planet, Abuhindra explained that as the Earth breathes, it must be fed the correct amount of water and air to bring a mist to its core.

For that to happen his team draw the reserve water from the rocks and develop the humidity that can dampen within the Earth, and so prevent the fire from growing uncontrollably. If that weren't done it would mean the end of the planet, or certainly the beginning of the end.

So, they collect the water that seeps through the rocks, and then flows through underground channels.

When it's untainted, that's fine, but when chemicals have seeped into the water, it becomes deeply worrying because that can then cause an explosion on the core, and make it unstable.

He finished by emphasising how harmful this is to the planet, and how he really hopes that the human race would soon find a viable alternative.

Human Obsession

In a different writing, Abuhindra said that there are distinct signs which show that when many chemicals are used, and then combine with others in the normal waste, they're intensely corrosive and invasive to all wildlife as well as the ground itself.

But he had observed that humans seem obsessed by cleaning, and yet they cannot survive on a sterile planet, because they need a powerful immune system, but that's constantly compromised through the immense range of chemicals used throughout life here on Earth.

Back in 2011, Esquaygo had also said that there was a time coming, where they'd need to challenge those who still feel there is nothing wrong in abusing Planet Earth; and that it has such fruitful resources, but they'll be lost through devastation.

He added that the Creator (God) didn't intend this to happen, and that it was mankind who created the problem, and brought such devastating brutality to the Earth that it was then incapable of moving on to a stronger base.

He warned that we had to be ready to bring about change in the need for good, and that mankind needed to commit to repairing what has become a devastated Earth and remove the impact of such chemicals and sound-based damage, so that it can then bring about a better future for the planet.

Moving Forward In A Positive Way

There's an old saying that 'The onlooker sees the game'. I don't know that the world has ever realised how many powerful onlookers are bearing witness to our destructive ways and ignorance.

'There are many directions in which the human race can bring a balance of proportions to the world and allow the actual planet to grow again.' This was the positive way that Abuhindra directed the conversation in 2019.

He said that it's worthwhile to Earth if we bring a balance to our lives, because it gives us a power of authority that we can't see or feel, but it's there to equip our minds, and bring peace to the soul, so that the future can be a balanced one.

Through the work of all those who love and cherish the soul of the Earth there's a loving energy that desires peace throughout.

He then explained that although the basic need of the Earth is hydrogen, it also carries metals and there's an entire layer of gold throughout its core which brings balanced growth. This then acts in a way of resourcefully bringing metal to metal which allows a chemical fusion that can in turn cause a great amount of energy.

It then holds that energy within, providing a colossal strength to which is added the gold particles spat out by the colossal force of the fire within.

The result is that it doesn't erode the planet's amount of power, but instead builds a core strength that can allow it to bring a positive energy and radiate good for everyone to consume, and benefit from. But the power isn't being used for its real purposes.

He finished by saying that if they move their focus from the Earth's power to that of the people, they will find that the ones who develop it, do so in a more upsetting way, using judgement, and misrule.

So, if instead, they balance the needed strength of the Earth and mankind, then future generations can benefit fully.

Chapter Seven: Healing, Balancing Life

Including: Developing Your Life Journey; Speaking Personally; Moving Forward Powerfully; Can Change Benefit Us As A Race; Speaking Personally; A Difficult Journey; Speaking Personally; Life The Leveller; Unconditional Love; Side Effects Of A Pandemic; We Are Custodians And Not Owners; Changing Our Vision Of God; Healing The World; Healing Earth's Pain; If Humanity Rejects Change God Will Make It Happen; Accepting Change; Speaking Personally; Joining A Universal Alliance; My Request To You; Finally.

Developing Your Life Journey

This is the point where some may say, 'Do everything my way and you'll have the formula for both your success and a healthy planet.'

But one element of this life journey which should be obvious to you now is that each formula has its own quirky uniqueness. Some of that depends on the original blueprint, but some also depends on the way you've developed it over lifetimes on Earth. We may share certain elements of soul development, but each package is individual so our goals may differ just as our skills do. Having said that, when we work together we form a team that can succeed.

Sad to say, there are many people who fear stepping out on their own in case they make mistakes, and yet those errors of judgement can provide their most potent lessons and strengthen their understanding.

But even if someone else launches a guaranteed way for others to follow, success is in the detail, and you may offer valuable development, which is also important. For at whatever level, whether on a planet or in Spirit, you're developing and that is vital for the future of all races and the planets themselves. But that development must be positive and beneficial to everyone.

There's something special about discovering your own power, and I know that with the information I've given you, that you can succeed. However, I also know that there are two important constants that you can't leave out of this winning life formula.

One is your soul, and the other is God.

So, when you ask where to start the process, my answer is unswervingly,

'Start by plugging into the Power Source.' That's God by whatever Name you use.

I'm being perfectly serious here because the difference it will make is immense.

It'll raise you to a higher level and that's exactly what you need. At the same time, it'll add another dimension of guidance and power that's tailored purely to your needs.

I'm not talking about getting religious, although I do understand that it's the route for some people. But always remember that religion's effectiveness depends on the quality of those who deliver God's messages. They may dominate with their advertising but ensure that they follow that up with a clear and true understanding of God. Some will be outstanding, some may not.

On the other hand, when you enjoy your own One to One relationship with God, you receive the understanding that's relevant to you and your personal journey.

- *Look on your conscience as a handbook for life.* If you're not sure whether you should or shouldn't do something, refer to your handbook. Does your conscience feel okay about it? Would you feel right or wrong doing it?
- *Once you're online with God you'll find that your inner satnav is also up and running.* It may be a gradual process learning to work with that guidance, but the more you do, the greater the value you'll find and develop in all parts of your life.
- *Chat to God, talk about your day, and ask for help to do things.* If you're afraid people will order an ambulance and two men in white coats if they see you talking to yourself too often, then hold your cell phone, and say you're talking to a friend. It's no lie.

Speaking Personally, like many of us I can still get the odd day when I get a big grey cloud hanging over me. I feel down but I don't know why, and it just makes me think that I can't achieve anything, no matter how simple.

So, I talk to God, and I tell Him how I feel, and that I need to regain my focus so that my day will shape up for me. I ask for His help and say that I really need it. Within two to three hours, I know the cloud will clear. It never fails.

Moving Forward Powerfully

I hope that I've shown in the preceding chapters that no matter who you are, you're here on Earth both to learn, and also to use that experience to understand and contribute to a better and healthier world.

We talk about evolution with animals and the landscape, but we don't include ourselves in this. However, as a race, we have challenges ahead which must conform now to a more peaceful and caring existence if we are to support the healing programme for humanity and the planet. This is a time of particularly hard lessons for all of us. They may vary a great deal, but they'll be appropriate to our needs.

We may not have come with a wish to harm the planet or to flood it with the world's currency, but, speaking as a member of the human race, that's exactly what we've achieved, because we've focused on our own needs and development, and our blinkered vision has blinded us to the needs of others and those of the planet.

But we can't buy our way out of our responsibilities. We have a debt to pay, and for every day we ignore the need to change, that will grow bigger.

I've recently received so many channelled writings on how to go about saving the planet, and they all have one common denominator,

'A belief in God'

Once we have that, we receive the empowerment to achieve whatever's necessary through our particular skills. That's why it's so important that we nurture our individual abilities and bring together our skills and passion.

A belief in God probably registers low on many people's wish list but, Abuhindra explained that it's because of the declining belief in God, and the growing certainty that the human race is no longer answerable to **anyone** for its actions, that the real energy within the world has depleted, and is now less than half of what it should be.

Why would that happen? Well, it's because, currently humankind as a race has very limited knowledge and power, despite believing that *we are the power*.

We're only accepting part of the overall picture, and that's not enough to handle our responsibilities in the world, let alone the Universe.

Abuhindra added that when there's a need for power to be given, God will provide it and that's part of His service to us. The problem is that when the human race isn't showing its own true power, it can't automatically be supplemented by God. There has to be a reason for Him to give it.

Also, when nature revives, there's a power that comes from the Earth too, but at the moment that's at a low ebb, so we're totally reliant on God's Power to provide the help. The crux is that we must show a ***need*** for Him to give it.

Currently, we're following a human led scientific resolve to heal Climate Change.

That's great! But this isn't the time for choosing either version 'a or b'. We must widen our vision and realise that although proof is a convincing persuader in some cases, we must balance that with trust for the areas beyond our current understanding. We must have faith, because only then can we employ the extra forces available to us through our souls, and at the same time heighten our knowledge and skills to a completely new level.

When we do, we become open to new possibilities, and we broaden our power by doing so.

We're already equipped with a link to God's Power and guidance. Now it's time to switch on the equipment.

A belief in God is like injecting the air we breathe with a powerful catalyst that clears the fog from our eyes, and allows us to see, and understand more. At the same time, it encourages us to work and live in a more caring and loving way.

It allows us to feel the joy of knowing we're helping to repair our planet, that it's safe and recovering well, and that the generations ahead can build on our powerful foundations and avoid the mistakes.

So, the formula we need to adjust to for a truly effective life includes guidance and empowerment from spirit power, as it will widen our vision, raise our expectation, empower us through unconditional love, and guide us through instinct and intuition.

With God as our guide, we can and will attend to all the needs of the world in the right order, and in ways that we haven't before contemplated.

Can Change Benefit Us As a Race?

If we're to survive as a race, this lust for terrorism, war and abuse must end. We can live better lives if we work together.

Then, maybe we can clasp hands across the world in love and respect. It's then that we'll be able to know again a vibrant and powerful future.

But we haven't reached that level of positivity yet.

So, the question is:

Does humankind need to change the way it lives, and bear the responsibility of healing all aspects of life, including its own people, the animal kingdom, and the planet itself?

The answer is: Yes, definitely!

As a race, we have deviated far from our expected journey in life, because we've been sold values that judge us more on how much money we have in the bank, rather than how much love we have in our hearts.

It's a bonus if we have both, but at the end of it, money is simply a tool, and it's not how much we have that impresses God. It's how we share our good luck, and the gifts that power us on. When that goodness flows an extra power is given by God.

It's hard to tell someone who's finding it difficult to meet their bills, that love is more powerful than money. Instead, we need to demonstrate it by showing the compassion that will help them find a stronger foothold in life.

And as we continue to face problems set in place by the Coronavirus pandemic, and then another war in

Europe, many more people who have never relied before on others for help, are now crying out for it. And it's the richness of people's hearts that will need to answer them.

It was on the 19th December 2019, that Abuhindra told me that a time of change was coming, and within three months many of us were in lockdown due to the Coronavirus.

He spoke of a time ahead that would bring devastation for those who clung to their savings and made no effort to help others to prosper. He said that many who believed their savings were protected, would instead be declaring bankruptcy; adding that the world had to learn a way of belief rather than money, and tend for the weak so that they could feel at one with the future.

Speaking Personally, I remember TV news covering the queues for foodbanks and seeing drivers of BMWs, Mercedes and other expensive cars waiting their turn. It's given us the understanding that so much that we have previously taken for granted can no longer be so.

But it's also the passion to help the vulnerable and needy that counts, and that becomes the catalyst that makes us act in a more caring and responsible way. Sometimes it's that memory of hardship that fires us with a need to help others. We resonate with those who are suffering, because we've lived through that lack of security, and we know the fear that goes with it.

Most of those alive now were born after the Second World War, and so Russia's War against Ukraine threatens life in ways beyond our imagination. More and more need help, and shelter. There are no winners in war, and while the human race fights, the planet does too… for its survival.

A Difficult Journey

We came to this life to learn and develop. Part of that is to be the helper, and the other part is as the receiver.

We must learn both skills; the power to give our best, and the humility of saying at times, 'Yes please, I need help'.

Admittedly, we chose a tough journey here on Earth, and for this generation and beyond it's tougher because we must heal the wounds that now threaten the life of the planet and all those that inhabit it. We may not be responsible for all the pain caused but we've readily built on it. And there's no Band-Aid big enough.

This life is harder for some than others, but then, although an owner's manual might in some ways be handy, we did come equipped for it, and added to that, we have a wonderful support team led by God, to guide and empower us all the way.

When I say that we're equipped it's because deep within us, we have a conscience that clearly allows us to recognise right from wrong, and when you follow that it helps you to act in a positive and caring way.

We also have a soul that's linked to God's Energy in the Spirit Realms so that when we work with our senses, our instincts /intuition, we're working with our soul's inner satnav. What better way to ensure that we are going to find and achieve a more powerful and rewarding life?

Speaking Personally, during my own journey here on Earth, I've experienced the restrictions that can come through conforming with modern society's desires, and I wish I had had the courage to work out whether my loyalties lay with me or the distant influences who pulled the strings.

But there are opportunities throughout our lives, when we suddenly get shaken to see if we're awake; and for me it was like an earthquake, because so much that I valued was threatening to slip away from me. But sometimes that's what we need, so for me it worked and suddenly I was awake and ready to change direction.

In the last 24 years, I've probably never worked so hard, or had so many adventures, or learned so much, or laughed so much, or felt love so intensely, not just for my husband, Mike or for our son, but for life itself, and for God's part in it.

Life the Leveller

The far-reaching effects of the Coronavirus pandemic has stunned many of us, along with the inadequacy of so many of the leaders in their efforts to protect their people. We see the way a virus can level classes as they join each other to queue for food, and we bless the way such emergencies can bring out areas of good and inspiring actions.

As we move on, it's now going to fall to everyone to play their part, and for people to show their goodness. But where difficulties and pain befall some, there are always certain areas of life that benefit, and I don't mean the funeral directors. What we have to do is make ourselves see how the balance of good can be maintained even after the problems ease.

For example, planet Earth benefited during lockdown simply as a result of the sudden lack of traffic both in the air and on the ground.

Pollution levels became much lower, and a little of the pain that we've inflicted each day on the planet eased for a while.

So, will this shake up awaken more people to the need to change their lives, because this isn't a situation we can ignore, and continue as if nothing has happened?

This is our time to move on. It's our opportunity to invest our love in a better future than we have contributed to in the past. But you may wonder what love can do.

Unconditional Love

Love is such an underrated power, and I'm talking here about unconditional love.

It's the powerful tool that you can use even when you don't like the person or people you're sending it to. They may have hurt you or offended you, but instead of ignoring them, you can send healing love and ask God to help them become better people.

Also, when you approach your day with love and respect, you help to smooth the ups and downs that come along, so that you can see the opportunities offered. I have to say from experience that it makes life flow more smoothly, and don't we all need that?

Side Effects of a Pandemic

I have learned that spirituality is also a code of conduct crucial to our practical life. That may seem strange, but I was taught early on in the focused area of my life with God that an important part is to help in the world. And why wouldn't we want to when we learn that it's not at a cost to us, but instead that it also benefits our life and development.

It's a shame that areas of humanity need to know what's in it for them before they'll help others, but that's the case with some who are just at the start of this powerful learning curve. Is it greed or insecurity? Either way, we must help each other to overcome that fear of losing out. After all, this is a situation where everyone gains.

Another concept where I believe we can lose some of the true meaning of life is if we get carried away with the theories of being an enlightened and good person but ignore the practicality of it.

Believe me when I say that God would prefer that we celebrate Him by helping the world to recover, and that includes the people, the animals, and the planet itself. When we are doing that, we're serving God, and He serves us by empowering and guiding each step we take.

Joining others in celebration of God can bring more to us than it does to God, because our commitment to Him is in making the world a better place and ensuring no one in need goes uncared for or hungry. Our actions show our love and respect for God when we truly care for our wonderful animal kingdom, and we nurture our beautiful planet. There are so many ways to do this, and it's a responsibility we all carry.

Self-development is necessary but not everyone can focus on spiritual skills like meditation, channelling, manifesting and the like, although they are positive and enjoyable ways to further some areas of growth. For those who don't wish to commit to that, their care and love can show in very simple, practical, and powerful ways by helping in the world.

There are many great exercises and tools, and I'm not diminishing them, but if they're to be worthwhile to us, we must use the power they bring us to help, not only ourselves, but others too. Because ultimately, they're there to guide us to put into action what we've learned and to use our skills at all levels to help others.

They furnish us with a way of caring for all life, restoring strength in the planet itself, and helping to build a better path for humanity as a whole. In other words, those are precious tools that simply guide us to work closer with our Power Source, God, act on the power given and revitalise our world for the future.

We can know that the guidance comes from our soul and God, and we can be assured that if we are alert to it, it will help us to achieve our goals. But those don't just concentrate on us as individuals, they bring other areas of need in the world into focus too.

I think we're at a point now where we need to return to some of our earlier understanding. We should throw out some of the self-promotion aspects of what we've been taught and realise that it's actually going to benefit our personal journey when we do positive stuff for others along the way. After all, we're here as part of a whole, and our positive input into life will make a difference, no matter how large or small it is.

We should also tear ourselves away from others' constant logic-based pathways and trust our own creative vision. When we follow our own instincts and inspirational thoughts, we become more powerful, and it can also be a lot more interesting.

In addition, we must relearn the value of respect. Whether it's for others, the world, God, life, or ourselves, it brings a more caring and tolerant attitude.

So, as we greet each day with love, forgiveness, and positivity, we can then experience the best it can give. After all, a new day is a fresh page turned in the Book of Life, and this is our chance to start a more powerful chapter in our history.

So, what's the first step in that new format?

We Are Custodians And Not Owners

We seem to have forgotten that we don't own the world, we are custodians, and that responsibility passes from one generation to the next.

The human race has grown a need to possess rather than share. Inhabiting with a view to improvement isn't enough. We've been taught to claim a piece of the planet, and we generally want a piece that's bigger than our neighbours'. We're even planning on claiming areas within space.

Ownership rates high in human terms particularly in developed countries. Yet, The White House and No 10. Downing Street aren't owned by their tenants. They come with the job, and once their role is over, they must vacate for the next tenant just as we must vacate for the next generation. But I see no loss of importance in being a tenant of either.

But whether, in human terms, we claim ownership with a legal document or we have a tenancy, it still leaves us with a clear responsibility to care and protect, and that means the planet as a whole. We came with the authority to protect and not abuse it. We must fulfil that.

I do feel that within this next chapter of life, we must give up any pretence of owning the planet, and accept with honour our duty of custodianship.

The world isn't ours to play and experiment with. We don't own our own countries, but we're responsible for their upkeep, we don't own other people's countries, but we do owe them the benefit of our care when they need help.

Instead of invading in order to govern, and satisfy the egos of a few, who care little for the people but revel in their own importance, we should meet in honesty and care. The world needs to work together if it's to change in the way needed.

Our planet won't survive with so much pain and negativity, so we must learn goodness and trust.

So, what's the next stage?

Changing Our Vision Of God

If we are to benefit from the wisdom and empowerment that will help us to reshape life, this is the time that we should see God as the amazing Creative Power this Spirit Force truly is.

If anyone should know what life is about, then it's God.

He created the original formula, and it was a winning one. The trouble is that sections of humanity have decided they can do a better job and have reprogrammed life with different goals that don't work.

But inevitably if you're not careful about what you put into a recipe, you can end up with a giant stomach ache, and I feel that I'm not alone in believing that both life and the planet are now experiencing the results of humanity's ignorance.

We each carry within us the 'equipment' and 'tools' to achieve a powerful and rewarding life, with or without financial riches. So much depends on not only what type of journey we chose for this life, but also balancing it properly.

We have the choice of joining others through religion to commit to God (by whatever Name we use), or as individuals to walk a more personal direction, which is the one that I prefer to follow. In that way we work directly with the Source.

After all, in practical terms, when possible, we plug into electricity for our electrical and technological equipment, so why wouldn't we use the Power Source available to us personally? When we do, we empower our lives to a level higher than before, and both our life journey and the planet benefit, with the knock-on effect that it strengthens the Universe.

The truth is that the more we use our own awareness through our instinctive and intuitive choices, the stronger and more gifted we become. We still need our brain's logic for other tasks, but we need to balance our intuitive side with its reasoning.

If we follow the scientific teachings, we reject anything that we can't prove, but part of our learning journey is to develop trust. How much do we lose by not doing so? Currently, we seem to be losing where we should be gaining, and the world is no happier for it.

I do feel that we have become a distrusting world. That leads to barriers, and we're quicker to find reasons to dislike rather than accept, so trust has no ground on which to build.

We're wary of changes, of people, of new things, of other planetary life, and of life itself.

But if we can't overcome our reluctance to trust, we shut the door on any help available to us, and yet we have never needed it more.

Trusting that there are spirit powers out there that can bring their understanding, and help us to move on, is the first step of a new and more powerful journey. Knowing that they are part of God's Team is reassurance that they're accredited, so by talking to God you learn the most effective way with the best operator.

Everyone develops their own way of connecting with God. It's just realising you can, and that it'll benefit every part of your life. You don't have to wait for someone to do it for you.

Yes, it can be a one-sided conversation, but I assure you, God is listening.

Healing the World
Healing comes in different ways.
You can heal with God's help –
- Just accept the natural process that allows you to work with instinctive guidance and inspiring thoughts that come through your soul, and God's Energy.
- The Spirit Plane and the Earth Plane are meant to work together, because then your life is more fulfilled, and you develop the good within the world as a whole.
- God has many helpers, and the angels, elementals and spirit guides wait to direct you along your particular path. They hate seeing you stumble and lose yourself in this demanding world. So, tell God of your needs and the help will be there. Without information, hints and guidance given by them, you are seriously underpowered. So, develop awareness, heed their guidance and be grateful for the help given.
- The Spirit Realms is intentionally contactable so that no one faces this difficult life alone. After all, your soul originally came from that plane for you to be born on Earth, and it'll return there when your human life is finally over, so that you can prepare for the next stage of repair and development.

- You can heal through being positive. When you focus on what you can do, rather than dwelling on what you can't, you achieve stronger results, and survive the difficult patches better.
- You can heal through forgiveness. Unforgiveness blinds you to the good in your life. It's like drip feeding poison on a plant. Gradually it loses its beauty and grows weaker.
- Forgiveness is the confidence of knowing that you learned from the situation, and stepped away, leaving those at fault to settle their own account of wrongs. It also means forgiving yourself, asking God for forgiveness, and learning from your mistake. (See the appropriate prayers in Section 3.)
- You can always heal through prayer. This is a powerful tool, and you should use it readily. (See the selection in Section 3)
- You can heal by touch. With unconditional love, you are equipped to heal, whether it's the person or their aura. Reassurance comes with a loving hand, or a hug, as does sympathy, and understanding.
- You can heal through your attitude. When you're positive, you find yourself looking for solutions to problems, whether it's for yourself or others.
- You can heal by offering help. Seeing a need and acting on it is love in action. By helping those who can't help themselves, you show you care.
- You can heal by helping others to feel better about life. That enables them to feel worthy and put more effort into their own lives.
- Words can heal. But there are also times when the most healing thing you can do is just listen.

The common denominator in all this healing is unconditional love. We're all capable of using that whether or not we like the person. Love is the power that can help heal both the victim and the perpetrator, and although you may not want to help those who hurt others, without that help they will continue to deliver pain. So healing is a positive energy to give.

But in the end, it's also remembering you can't make other people's choices for them. They have to find those that are right for them, just like you and I do.

Healing Earth's Pain

I do feel that although there are positive actions being taken by some responsible and far thinking people, and organisations scattered throughout the world, the Earth deserves our full attention and commitment, and if that's uncomfortable for those with other business agendas, then they will have to at some point begin responding to our planet's needs.

On one side, there's a growing number of people who already understand some of the areas of pain within the world, and they accept their responsibility as part of the human race, to make the changes necessary to both empower them and allow the planet to heal fully. They must be supported and encouraged because history will show that through their efforts, our world was brought back from the brink.

In the middle are those, who hang back because they believe that they are powerless to influence the changes, and that others must do it instead.

If you're one of those people, then sorry but you're wrong. Even your smallest efforts will contribute something good. Even if your job is to simply help the helpers.

On the other side there are those groups of people who've enjoyed or profited from the very products and practices that threaten the Earth's survival.

They may have created these in ignorance of the harm they would cause, but if their priority lies in ensuring that change doesn't harm them financially or affect the fabric of life that they have become used to, then this is the time for them to wake up and realise that in any species, those who don't evolve can't survive the changing factors that come from an altered planet.

Neither can we afford to ignore the potentially controversial subject of destructive military weapons. In an uncertain world, who would be the first nation to commit to disarming, but without changes the planet will continue its decline and its painful fight for survival.

If Humanity Rejects Change God Will Make It Happen

On the 11th November 2022, Abuhindra gave this warning.

'When the way of the world brings upset, there is a need for intervention, and that is when God is voracious in His thinking. He will bring a catalogue of disaster if it is necessary to reverse the thinking of mankind, and it will bring an upset so great that the world will have to reverse its way and bring goodness again.

But this has not been the way forward desired by God.

It has become the only way to reverse the upset brought on by those who don't care for a planet of great importance. And so, there is a time limit before it becomes necessary, however, it's the Power used when there is no other way.

So, abide now by the rules of God and there will be a future of wisdom, for the world. However, ignore it, and not only will the world suffer, but it will bring havoc to a way of life not sanctioned by God.'

I asked if the time limit was 600 years, and Abuhindra replied, 'It may be earlier if the way of the world is to continue its upset, but not earlier than 300 to 400 years.'

Accepting Change

To achieve change, we ***must*** as a race, wake up to the needs that lie outside our own, but also ultimately affect our future.

We have to build bridges rather than blow them up. We must alter the way we think, judge and act, which will then be a catalyst for overall change.

We need alliance rather than defiance. We also need to develop trust.

Speaking Personally, to be completely honest we all have our little comfort zones. They may not always be that comfortable, but they're familiar, and mentally we can hang on tight to the cliff edge, with white knuckles, and the ground falling away, but we are so scared of the consequence of change, we don't even imagine that there's a safety net to catch us.

Yet, when it eventually comes it may be life changing.

About 5 years ago, my husband Mike experienced a dire situation,.

He'd had kidney stone problems for quite a few years and after many operations, he'd lost one kidney because it was no longer viable. Dialysis had been mentioned along the way as the other kidney also had issues, but Mike was adamant. He would not go on dialysis. He saw it as the last step before death.

But sometimes you're pushed over that tipping point, and for us it was when his remaining kidney stopped working. It seemed as though the stones within had blocked it. He was building up fluids within him.

Suddenly he was on dialysis to ease the emergency. No discussion. Simply no option.

He's still on it and visits the clinic three times a week, and that's been life changing. But what it's taught us is that with a positive attitude you can work through necessary changes and enjoy a quality of life you hadn't expected. In fact, we are now so grateful for the dialysis clinic, because it's given Mike the ability to live a pretty normal life outside the treatment time, and without that he wouldn't even be here.

When change is the only option, no amount of complaining or resisting is going to make things better, in fact it'll only make things worse, because instead of planning and acting in a positive way, we're delaying.

So sometimes we must face up to change because, without it there's no future, but with it there can be fresh opportunities.

We don't always realise how powerful we are until these things happen. But one thing we mustn't forget is that whatever it is, God is always there to guide us.

Joining A Universal Alliance

On the 27th October 2021, Abuhindra spoke to me about the future of planet Earth within the Universe. He said there must be an alliance between the people on Earth and others throughout the Universe, and that there are many ways to bring peace and neutrality, but at the moment the human race is constantly on patrol, and it's looking to fight, so peace is unsustainable.

He added that although this is a planet at war, no one seems to recognise the damage it's bringing both to itself, and to its need for friendship and alliance throughout the Universe.

He then made a very clear statement,

'For there to be true dynamism in the world again, we must see less aggression and aggravation, and it must again be a hope that the world will join an alliance throughout the planetary Universe, and reverse its past thinking. For a future awaits of a powerful alliance between planets, and yet it cannot be that the Earth brings friendship if it cannot heal the wounds of the past.'

My Request to You

If you have found the whole or even part of this book illuminating and empowering, I hope that you will share that with others.

Some will readily understand, but you also need to include those who are not like you. I say that because, where you hopefully now recognise and accept a broader vision of our existence, others may still prefer a more filtered view which doesn't commit to change.

But if we are truly to save our race and our planet, we need them on board too, and those include the people whose first thoughts are, 'What's in it for me? Why should I change? How will it help me?

They're cautious, they disbelieve those who say, 'You must change the way you see life because it'll help the world', and in some ways I can't blame them. They've been taught that attitude for centuries. But clarity comes at different points.

When I was counselling a lifer in Prison, I worked through its chaplaincy. The chaplain remarked one day that the prison was a very negative place to work. He said that it was like the farmer spreading seed in his fields. Some of the seed falls on fertile ground, but a lot falls on the rocks and he said that you couldn't do anything there.

Immediately I was given the response, 'Yes but wait for the first shower and some will wash off the rocks onto the fertile ground.'

That was one day the prison chaplain didn't have an answer.

So, talk about this book to anyone who'll listen, because they may surprise you later.

The world may have widened its power technically, but in many ways our lives have become more insular.

My job was made clear to me in a regression over 20 years ago with Vernon Frost, when I heard my soul declare through my own voice that I am a Messenger for

God. My husband Mike was present as were others. At that time, I was humble and embarrassed. I had to prove to myself that I was worthy of the role. But now I have no hesitation in saying to you:

'God, all the Powers in Spirit, those on other planets and I, the Messenger say, 'Whoever you are, we need your help, and your support. We can become entrenched in our ways and flinch at change, but when we unite in our effort, we oil the wheels that make that journey easier and more successful.

We can't bring change alone. None of us can, but if we work with our neighbours, and our friends (wherever they are) we can succeed where before it seemed impossible.

So, I ask you now to put away any doubt, and to know that as we link arms to combat Climate Change, and act in the best way for the future to become a good one, we'll see a time ahead guaranteed for new generations; and that should be our aim.

Let's now share our life with the ones who will build a future for our children, and those who follow them. Let's bring kindness to Mother Earth and help her to retain her power and use that to help the human race succeed where before they failed.

So, if you know anyone who may benefit from reading this, then I ask for your help in reaching not just their minds, but more importantly, their souls.

Finally...

We can no longer afford to ignore the big picture. We can't say, 'But it doesn't affect me!'

Why would we want to, when we know that our positive actions can change the future and bring good to the world as well as our own development?

Never in the history of the human race has global peace meant so much to the survival of this planet and its inhabitants, and never before has it been so important that everyone plays their part.

We can't pretend that it'll be easy, but the longer we delay, the harder it will be to achieve.

Jesus once said to me that although this world has free will, there might be a time later when that won't be so.

On the 23rd August 2021, I asked Abuhindra this question.

'Will humanity remain free willed, or will it change?' I asked because I really do wonder how we will otherwise achieve peace throughout the world.

Abuhindra's answer was this, 'There is a need to believe at this time that the world will respond without added force to comply in the need for peace.

There is a need only to bring compliance if it is seen that there is no other way to stop a people from destroying itself. But I see no action to be taken for a number of years yet.

Maybe it will be so in 400 years or so, but I doubt it will be necessary. And God will decide if it is to be so.'

When you consider the situation of the human race on that other planet Earth so long ago, it's obvious that we were a more positive force. We handled life better there because there was a greater spiritual awareness among people. Surely, it must have been a more pleasurable experience!

The overall balance of life was maintained and that allowed all people to preserve the goodness of humanity which, in turn, led to a need to follow a more caring and respectful path. But we seem to have discarded that balance of understanding, and substituted our own version of the formula, which is unbalanced, and in many ways more destructive. It certainly can't achieve the goals we set ourselves. We can do better, and we need to.

We did it once! Why not again? By working together, we can bring back that balance, rebuild the power within life's formula, and strengthen our future.

Where before the planet has grown to know us through the pain we've inflicted, let's now introduce our healing side, and become the rescuers. Let's show it the compassion that it deserves as our cherished home.

For we have the potential to take forward life in a safe way, and that is so valuable. We also owe it to ourselves and the world to get this right, so let's work together and do it. Our future and that of the planet will depend on it.

Section Two

Developing and Shaping Your Life

Life Develops Like A River

A river emerges from the Earth as a tiny dribble of water slowly spreading out through its boggy beginnings.

This is your new life as a baby emerging from your mother's womb at the beginning of your life on Earth. Your purpose is 'to be', so you haven't found your flow yet and you rely on others completely. It grows to a small stream forming a path through the soft earth as pebbles obediently move to the side to accommodate it.

You are no longer the new-born. Suddenly your character is growing, and you have an identity. You're making a mark in the world, and the guidance from others is gentle.

The stream grows in size and forms a channel. Instinctively, it heads towards the sea. The riverbed becomes stonier and there are rocks that divert the flow. Ahead is a gorge, and as the water squeezes through, the force is great.

Over time you've grown into a young person who's making a mark in the world. The river's stones represent people who are trying to influence your flow in life. Your focus is being trained logically to succeed, so your choices are being narrowed. It's important that you don't lose the balance of your soul's instinct, and your heart's passion as they compete with your brain's need to dominate with logic. Don't get bruised by negative thoughts when positivity can guide you so much better.

The growing strength of the water digs deep and wide into the banks. The power of the river is growing.

You're starting to make a deeper mark, which means that you're beginning to leave a lasting impression on life.

The channel flows forward but now some people have interfered with the flow and dug a trench to change its direction, because they feel it will be beneficial to them as well as the surrounding area, and increase its value. They ignore the possible effect on valuable wildlife and plants.

There are those people who feel they know better than you, and they may force you to adopt their beliefs, understanding and direction in life. They may ignore your instinctive resistance. Gut feeling means nothing to them.

The river's flow has been disrupted. Many creatures rely on the water source and where it used to benefit fish and wildlife along the original path, it's been reclaimed and lies barren. Although the diversion leads back to the original further down the river's natural route, the force of the water is weaker, and the direction it's been forced to follow doesn't flow well.

Your life may have been manoeuvred by those who believe that your choices were poor compared with their options, and they may continue to divert you. Will you be persuaded by them or pursue what you instinctively feel is right?

If it's lucky there will be wiser people later who will study maps and say 'This river didn't originally follow this direction. Let's reintroduce the wild animals that used to guide the flow so that it benefited more areas, because this river has a powerful flow that can greatly improve our environment like it used to. We need beavers, then our woods will be healthy again, and the insects will come back which will bring back the smaller animals and birds.'

There are people who recognise a more instinctive way to follow life, and they feel right. With their help and guidance, you can regain your true power and help others physically, emotionally, and instinctively.

The river's strong flow is now beautiful to see. It's grown wide. It inspires far seeing people to construct weirs and water wheels that will help locals to share in its power and help industry and the environment; and the river is happy to contribute. However, it doesn't enjoy the growing taste of plastic, and rusting metal that come from discarded bags, prams, and supermarket trolleys. It affects the fish, and some float lifeless on the surface. Larger items ensnare wildlife, and rubbish is everywhere, collecting dirt, and mould, and then infecting the water with sewage and factory waste.

Your life speeds up as you try to become this powerful person. Rubbish food may be wrapped beautifully but can't help you stay healthy. You may think that others know the best route for your life, your diet, your friends, and your interests, but do they? You're an individual and your needs may not be the same as theirs. Don't compromise.

Areas of water begin to cut into the land and many people use it as irrigation. That's positive. Inevitably some others will not recognise the value of the water and they leave areas to become stagnant.

There are those people along the way whom you inspire and then there are those who will drain your energy because they demand too much. Ensure that you are protected.

At last, the river can detect the sea is not far now and it can then be free to spread its goodness.

Your life on Earth is drawing to an end, you know that God's beckoning your spirit to join others, who have survived the ordeals of a human life and are ready to head home to The Spirit Realms. Like you, some others have suffered areas of life where their dreams became spoilt.

The sea is already filtering in, and the river knows it's where it belongs. Yes some people have littered the water there too, but healing awaits. It's important to believe in the power of the river and that, with help, it can regain the strength it was given by God's Energy. It relaxes into the flow of the sea. It feels right here. God's Authority reigns strongly.

Your time on Earth is waning. Your spirit is being called home and just as a butterfly sheds its pupa, your soul shakes free of its mortal costume and flies free to the place where all homeward bound souls gather. The Spirit Realms offer you tranquillity. Only those who chose a destructive life need to quake. Your journey is far less daunting. You're home, but work is not over. You must now increase your strength and move on. Of course, God and His Team are there to help you.

Life Changing Steps

To help you on your life changing journey, this section offers exercises and changes to your routine that will guide you to grow in a positive and powerful way. Remember knowledge is only part of the journey. Working with it is enables change to happen.

It provides a variety of ways to power up your life. This includes simple exercises, routine changes, and 'out of the box' ideas that can colour up your day and help you to achieve that elusive feel-good factor. No matter where you are in life, you can benefit.

In Section 3 there's a selection of life changing tools and prayers which you can also use. They were given by God for me to share with you.

Routine Changes And Exercises Including: The Importance of Communicating Daily With God; Optimise Your Life; Finding Life's Purpose; Guidance, Your Life Changer; An Exercise In Forgiving; Unconditional Love, A Natural Partner To Forgiveness; Get Your Mind, Body, And Spirit Primed For Take Off; Nourish Your Mind And Body; Explore The Natural Power Of Colour; Crystals; Declutter Your Life; The Power Of Contemplation; De-Stress; Two Earth Exercises To Relax And Revitalise; Become You; Care For Your Soul; Be An Achiever.

Some information is deliberately short, in order to whet your appetite. There are other books on the subjects, so research them. This is the part where *you* take action to improve your life and play your part in the world. After all, knowledge can widen your understanding, but only action can build the structures of a more powerful life. So, let's get started.

The Importance Of Communicating Daily With God

Because God is a vital part of your life, I have listed this as a priority. So, ensure you make space in your day to share with this incredibly Powerful Spirit Being.

You don't have to be well dressed to talk to God. You can be in work overalls, or lounging on the settee. God doesn't mind.

Personally Speaking, I remember being invited to attend an important service in a Cathedral in Serbia, and while I stood there, some people came in late and stayed for five or ten minutes to listen, pray, and light a candle. There was a woman with a toddler, working people in overalls, as well as housewives dressed for their daily tasks. No one stared or judged them. I felt it was how God would want it.

To truly empower your life, you must be ready to accommodate changes in your day. Build a routine that includes a daily chat with God and use prayer on a regular basis. You'll notice that some of the prayers that God gave me to share with you in Section Three also act as an affirmation. Where they start with 'I am ready to', the more you say them, the more you will help yourself to realise the power you already hold within you. That will then take you on to greater strengths and understanding.

Why is this so important?

Because God is part of the Foundation of Life. Without His intervention, life's true structure is lost, development is less, and the planet will become uninhabitable. So, your communication builds the first stage of an important relationship with God and a powerful step towards saving the planet.

How to begin:

Prayer is the recognised way of communicating with God, but it's also good to **Chat**.

Maybe, at the beginning you won't talk about things freely, but after a while you'll feel more relaxed and include personal things that concern you in some way.

When you chat with God you replace the distant vision of this immense Spirit Power with a working relationship. Together you can become a special team. That doesn't diminish the respect between you, but it allows more to be achieved.

You can talk frankly as in this example:

'Hello God, I know I haven't talked like this before, but I am trying to make changes, and this is one of them. I've had a bad time recently, but you already know that. You may have wondered why I didn't ask for help.

Well, I've always tried to sort things out myself, but not always successfully. I know you won't solve things for me, but I realise you can guide me to better solutions. Please, I need your help.'

When you talk to God, help comes in ways that are appropriate to your need. The angels may help, or spirit guides, or even elementals. But remember:

- God needs you to be honest with Him.
- You should recognise the good in your day and build on the positives. Good things happen, even in bad days.
- Whatever positive changes are needed, you should be willing to action them.
- *You* may feel specific changes would resolve your problems, but while you see the immediate future, God sees further, so your short-term solution may be wrong long-term!
- You may want something that works now, but you should understand that God will work in whatever way fits in with your overall needs, so that positive opportunities are there for you.
- When change isn't possible, He'll strengthen you and help you to cope. **He won't ignore you.**

Personally Speaking, I'm reminded of an elderly man who came to me in Glastonbury for guidance when Jesus was my Spirit Guide. He asked some questions and received clear answers, but you could see that he had something specific that was bothering him, and he was struggling with his words. Then suddenly as he got up to leave, he burst into tears and asked the question he really needed answering. He'd been hoping I would broach the subject for him, but Jesus knew he had to break through that difficult barrier. Once answered, he left happy. It made me realise that God needs to know that we recognise our situation and will act when there's a need.

Use Prayer

As well as chatting to God and sharing day-to-day issues and joys, it's also very powerful to pray.

Prayer is a valuable tool, but don't say it in a religious way. God needs to hear from *you* personally, so be natural.

Simply ensure that:
a) The prayer is true, sincere, and in your own words.
b) Say it in a positive way. Don't sound bored or defeated. When you're talking to God, there's no reason to feel defeatist!

Prayer is your *most powerful tool.* But don't forget to include the world's needs too.

As you relax into your prayers you may well find that words are suggested to you. Use them if they feel right.

Conversations aren't one-sided, but it's important to understand how God may respond.

God reaches you through your soul, so in order to fully appreciate His help, you need to become more aware. Your sixth sense is there but has probably become dulled because you've been taught to rely on other people's expertise to guide you.

Imagine a group of experts choosing the perfect wine for your meal. You may taste it and find it too dry or too sweet for your palate. Just as your sense of taste is unique to you, so is your inner guidance.

If someone tells you that you need to do something, allow your senses to tell you first whether or not it feels right. Your instincts and gut feeling will relay your own soul's guidance and it's reliable because through it, you're connected to God.

Consider it for too long and you'll have second thoughts. That's your brain's logic trying to override your first choice. It has limited understanding and if you allow it, it'll be like letting the wine expert choose your wine. So, don't.

We should learn from the example of animals because they still use their instincts, but the human race has been wrongly persuaded that it can have a vastly superior intelligence by focusing on brain development, and when you close the door on valuable instinct, and intuitive thought, it creates an imbalance that can't be compensated for by your brain.

It's a modern human trait, throwing out the old and replacing it with a new version. Weight of opinion tells us it's the right thing to do, so we follow blindly, and at a cost, because our brain alone won't show us the whole picture, and without a true balance we can't make decisions. We still trust senses such as sight, sound, smell, feel and taste, but science has taught us to reject our inner satnav, the soul.

Where God offers:

God's guidance+ Brain logic + Soul understanding = Powerful Mind, and Spirit directional guidance

The Human Race offers:

Brain Logic alone = Inadequate Mind directed guidance.

The human mind judges your abilities according to your experiences in your current life.

The soul is aware of what you've achieved prior to this life. With the power of your soul and your mind, your life becomes more dynamic, and you work smarter. But at the beginning you may have to work on those soul 'muscles' to get them flexing again. It's worth it, because there can be some situations that demand fast responses, and if your brain rules, you may still be on the starting blocks, asking 'Are you sure?' while others who trust their senses are part way down the track.

Follow Your Instincts

If someone snapped their fingers and asked you what you felt instinctively, could you answer them? This skill has always been there for you, but maybe it's dulled.

Faced with a threatening animal in centuries gone by, you wouldn't have considered whether to pat it on the nose and make friends! No, the hairs on the back of your neck would have been standing to attention, your psychic sense would have been signalling 'Need to go!' and you would be responding by looking for ways to escape. Those were your instincts, and they instantly assessed the situation and gave you a clear signal. Sadly, most of us have been 'taught out' of using one of our most powerful tools, because instincts were our guide long before we learnt to override them with reason. Many high achievers in our modern world work instinctively, so join them by sharpening this valuable way of sensing, because as you get used to instinctive decision making, you'll help life to deliver a positive and true meaning.

After all, your soul is a treasure chest of knowledge, gleaned from your previous experiences, so your instincts can help you to recognise when something is good as well as when it's not.

Soul Inspiration + Mind Planning + Action = Positive Results

Watch instinctively for trends, coincidences, and repeated information that points you in a particular direction, for life's synchronisation allows opportunities to open up, and lead you forward. So, take notice of that interesting advert that keeps cropping up, and don't ignore things like a niggling thought that you should change your diet.

Include God in Your Day

'I haven't got time' won't work anymore. If moving forward with your life means enough to you, you **will**

find time to include the exercises and tools that will help you to improve your day and build growth. Find time to:
a) Chat to God in the car, in the shower, or when you're washing dishes. You can always find opportunities when you need to, it doesn't have to be in a place of worship. God's aware of the pressures on your time, and will make your chat a priority if He sees you doing so.
b) Say a simple daily round up prayer, where you talk about the day and ask for help for yourself, other people, animals, and anything else that's important.

Always say 'Thank You' Be grateful for the help given to you. You'll benefit too when you become more appreciative, so don't take things for granted.

Optimise Your Life

There has never been a more crucial time to play your part in the world, but to do that you must first rediscover those skills that you've either forgotten or haven't been aware of. They're there for you to use, and they can help you to be more inspired and in control of your life as a whole.

Wherever you currently are in life, ***this is your starting point.*** It's where you begin to focus on what you can do, rather than what you can't.

Take Some Simple Life Changing Steps.

At this stage you should have with you a small notepad or your mobile's Notes App to jot down those inspirational thoughts that grab your attention. You don't know when they'll fly in, so always be prepared. That way you're planting the ideas you need to build on, using those guiding instincts to develop your life of purpose.

Plan how you can integrate something extra into your life, then don't be put off. Simply realise that if you're meant to do it, an opportunity will arise that you can work with. You may need to prioritise your day, but if you ask, you'll receive guidance in the form of inspiration and ideas, and you can work it out from there.

Changes don't happen without action so don't make the mistake of just thinking, 'If I want this enough it'll happen.' No, it won't without *your* input.

See it as something you *need* because it really is, so you should do everything you can to make it work. Why? Well, it's going to help you to grow your understanding. It's going to benefit you in every part of your life, and you'll also fulfil your need to help somehow in the world.

Don't be put off by positive ideas just because you wouldn't have previously considered them. If they're worthwhile, get involved. Some guidance may take you well outside your comfort zone, getting you involved in things that you've admired others for doing but never dreamed of doing yourself; but it's part of your learning journey, so give it your best. As you grow bolder, the joy you get from achieving, and helping in the world will motivate you to do more.

Step 1. If you already have a passion that you need to act on in life, then make enquiries about achieving it.

Does it mean a change of career, or is it something that you can develop alongside your existing work?

Does it involve personal training as an interpreter, a chiropractor, a Reiki or Spiritual Healer, an extension of your existing work, or some other skill? If so, feel the excitement of a new direction and make enquiries.

Do you want to....
- Help or maybe start a charity? If so, get the relevant information and do it.
- Do you want to help wannabe cooks to find their way around the kitchen and cook for their family? It's a valuable thing to do at this time, where many people are having to develop new skills in order to live more cheaply and healthily.

- Maybe you can upcycle or repair household furniture and machinery. The most practical of tasks can help the world to recover and when you do that, you're not just working practically, you're also understanding spiritually the needs of the planet, and God will help anyone who heals rather than destroys.
- Do you feel a deep need to sail around the world and raise funds for a charity at the same time? If so, start checking out sailing clubs.

This is a short list of possibilities, but you can see what I mean. Just start making enquiries and don't be put off. You're an explorer and entrepreneur now.

Of course, there'll be challenges ahead but follow your gut feeling. If it feels right, then work out how to overcome them. Sometimes compromises must be made, but once things have started, your enthusiasm will help you to do what it takes so that you can develop the power needed for your journey.

Step 2 is to recognise that your personal challenges may put a wedge between you and friends and some family members, who may not understand why you're doing this, and will think you've mentally fallen off the planet!

But this is about *you,* so just be determined and stick to your dream. Commit to it. If you are to fulfil an ambition you have to be single minded. It's that entrepreneurial determination that helps you to succeed!

Some will understand and admire you, but others won't. There'll also be those who'll try to make you feel guilty, because they don't like change, and it may affect them, but then you'll probably attract many others who will feed off your enthusiasm and take steps to follow your lead.

So, ask God to help you to stay strong and determined, so that you can achieve your goals.

Step 3 is to turn your thoughts and ideas into ***actions***, because that's where you start achieving. Yes, it can be scary stepping outside your comfort zone at the beginning, but take it one step at a time and, you'll find that each one feels right, and your confidence is growing. As the worry of getting lost within an open environment eases away from you, life will soon start to take on a greater meaning.

Speaking Personally, By the time I realised the importance of stepping out of the conformity lane on life's highway, and taking a different route, I was a wife and mother, and also acting as a carer for my own partially disabled, alcoholic mother. But I was fortunate because my husband Mike was supportive, in fact he enjoyed getting involved too.

My early journey of development threw challenges at me, especially when I remarked 'I could never do that…….' Within weeks there I was, facing it. My goodness, that did stretch me! It took me way outside my comfort zone, and forced me to learn, and although some of those lessons were uncomfortable, they had their value, and later I appreciated how much stronger and determined I'd become as a result. I gained precious understanding. I also learned not to say, 'I could never that!'

I knew I had God on my side and although some situations forced me to face issues that I would have preferred to avoid, it also made me release myself from many restrictive views I had been taught when I was younger; so, each time I emerged a little freer, a bit stronger, somewhat wiser, and a lot more honest with myself. I can truly say that I was a lot happier with the person I was becoming, and life was shaping up to be so much more rewarding.

I have learned that the 'honest' bit is important, because how can you be the real 'you' if you paint a false picture of yourself and your intentions. Until you do, you're simply preventing the free flow of positive energy.

Cherish Yourself

When you face new situations with the confidence that comes from experience and understanding, you can see positive opportunities that you maybe wouldn't have noticed beforehand. Your learning grows and mixes with the good that's already within you, and you learn to cherish and care about yourself. And that's important, because how can you be strong for others who need you, if you're not strong for yourself?

You may have made many mistakes in the past and maybe you hurt people. We all do. But when you develop a positive and unconditionally loving pathway and then you ask forgiveness for your poor decisions in the past, you gain a stronger and more positive understanding, and *that* is the person that you become.

Finding Life's Purpose

Your life's real purpose can reveal itself over time. For instance, if you had told me 25 years ago that mine would be working with God, I wouldn't have believed you.

So don't expect an immediate answer like, 'You'll be the first human to land on Mars'.

The answer will probably unfold bit by bit like layers of wrapping paper over something precious.

There are two basic routes you can take to find your life's purpose but, whichever way you choose, the information will come from your soul.

One Way (Develop with others)

You could find a spiritualist church or centre and use their development workshops and meditation groups to grow your awareness of the natural link you have with spirit and God.

It's all there, and I can confirm it's a fascinating journey to take. I trained first as a spiritual healer and then went on from there. You don't have to be a church member, and there's a lot of skills to learn as you develop your awareness. It can take you on an unexpected and enriching journey, and at the same time, it can open new areas of life to you.

But that direction isn't for everyone, and anyway, God would not have devised a programme where every person on the planet had to learn advanced skills, so that they could understand what area of development to pursue to achieve their true purpose.

A Second Way (A Home-Based Method)

Because this has become an era of science and technology, the focus of learning has been on developing the brain, and, over time we have become less and less aware of our soul's natural signals.

So, this is a gradual process of ***relearning*** the awareness with which you were born. Everyone should have the freedom and ability to do this, and it can become part of your day, naturally, although at the beginning you need to focus more carefully on what *you're* doing, or you'll miss things.

So, arm yourself with a pen and pad, take ten to fifteen minutes from your busy day, and lock yourself in the bathroom or in the car so that you don't get disturbed.

First you need to relax your body, and then, the big challenge... try to quieten your busy brain. This is where meditation can come in handy, so if you can join a meditation group, it can help you in different ways.

If the battle of the brain is too much, then as you relax, allow yourself to daydream, because that'll help take you to a comfortable place and shift your focus from those interfering daily thoughts.

Once you feel yourself winding down, tap into a favourite memory and completely immerse yourself in it. By that I mean see it, hear it, feel it, taste it, and smell it.

My own special memory is of a visit to Coronado Beach near San Diego. I was walking along the edge of the Pacific Ocean, and the warm waves were lapping over my feet and swishing away the sand beneath them. It felt wonderful.

When I go on that journey in my mind, within those moments, I **feel** the warmth of the water between my toes, and the sand easing away on each step. I **see** the beauty of my surroundings, I **hear** the soft sound of breaking waves, and **taste** the saltiness of the sea on my lips. I enjoy the unique **smell** of the seaside and the sun on my back. It relaxes me completely, and I'm so immersed that it clears my busy mind.

Get yourself to that relaxed space and then note down those inspirational and instinctive thoughts that fly in. They may be single word thoughts, ideas, or even reminders about a health issue.

You may have to practice a bit at the beginning but write down all your positive thoughts and ideas. What about those nagging ones that have been at the back of your mind? Any negative ones aren't from God, so don't be fearful that you'll get it wrong.

Become aware of your gut feeling. When you need to plan, be aware of that feeling in your stomach area. Does it feel comfortable about going ahead, or does it make you feel uncomfortable?

It directs you to where you need to be. It also confirms to you whether something or someone is good for you, or not and that allows you to know the correct step to take.

You will have been aware of your five senses...... Taste, Touch, Sound, Sight, and Smell, but the sixth one that unites you with your soul, has been sacrificed, because it doesn't tell you why you need to do something.

The brain always *needs* to know why, and we have increasingly been taught to always ask the reason for something. But to enjoy a more productive life we need to be in better balance, and we achieve that by employing both the brain and the soul and growing that magic ingredient called 'trust'.

I have found with my own guidance that it's not necessary to ask 'Why? Why do I need to do this?'. You'll learn the answer to that later. Instead, if you're unsure how to start, then ask, 'How? How do I start? How do I work this into my day?' And then step into uncharted territory with your soul's inner satnav.

Become aware of the pointers in this treasure hunt called 'Life':

- Maybe the newspaper or directory that falls open at a point which aligns with those earlier thoughts.
- Possibly it was when someone mentioned how they set about something similar.
- Could it be the business card you didn't dismiss, but instead put in the drawer, just in case....
- Allow yourself to follow the positive directions offered to you.
- Be prepared to put the effort into this new opportunity.
- Be ready to step outside your comfort zone.
- Be patient and don't give up at the first difficulty. This will take practice.

One of my earliest areas of guidance was to work with offenders. I'd been taught to believe that justice was as clear cut as black and white, and that in some cases, when criminals were locked up, they should stay there.

I arranged to regularly visit a local prison and help a lifer who'd been there for 22 years. I learned that around a quarter of offenders were illiterate and so ended up committing crimes. I also signed up as a volunteer with Probation. It was an amazing experience which taught me so much, but it took a bit of courage to take that first step. I'm so glad I did. It was so rewarding.

Following your soul's direction, you'll gradually discard the teachings that don't fit you well, and you'll adopt the ones that do, and that will help you to feel better about yourself. After all, you're being honest.

An important part of our learning journey is helping others. We gain from doing so, and we shouldn't take from the world without giving back.

So, don't write off any inspiring thoughts, because they're there to guide you towards your optimum direction.

Always remember that God's Spirit Energy understands that you must also fulfil the practicalities of life, so you'll receive the nudges that help you to maintain a powerful route forward. They may be:

- About your health: Maybe it's a reminder that you were going to talk to the pharmacist or doctor about that pain.
- About your diet: Food intolerance, allergies, or other dietary changes may be the focus.
- About helping in the world: Maybe you'll consider using your practical skills to help at a local wildlife centre or at a food bank. There are many opportunities, where they're desperate for volunteers.
- About relaxing into a new and unexplored interest: What about finding more 'Me Time'. Maybe developing art or writing skills.

These are just a few examples of how your soul can guide you to balance and fulfil your life, but whatever it's telling you, remember that to make any difference *you must act on them!*

Always understand that both you and God need you to be strong so that you're able to operate more efficiently, so don't run yourself ragged.

It may take a bit longer to get comfortable with your life journey along The Second Way, but you have a lifetime to nurture and feed it. So, don't be put off. You need the staying power of an entrepreneur. Simply know that it'll work.

Guidance, Your Life Changer

Life's guidance will reach out to you, but will you see it or accept it? Never fear the help that's offered when it's positive. It can be from people that you don't expect.

Of course, it isn't there purely to take you down the pretty pathways in life. There'll be times where you won't want to take that first step that you ***know*** is necessary, but you must. I know because I've been there.

There are times where your spiritual guidance will take you down a practical path. It may be a painful situation that you don't want to talk about, but it's important to do so if that is where you're guided, because your action will open the first stage of healing the situation, so that positive change can follow, and it's then that the path can become easier.

Refuse to take that step and you'll prolong the pain and possibly make it worse. When something is blocking your path, the only option is to move it out of the way, so that you can go forward. Strengthen your will, and you will empower your life.

Learn to Recognise Guidance

Your inner satnav is working but how will ***you*** recognise the messages?

Think of life as a treasure hunt and you won't be far out. It can offer challenges, and the inevitable forfeits for when you get it wrong, but it'll also offer prizes when you get it right; and the more you tune in to the simpler clues along the way, the better you'll do and the more you'll achieve.

    a) What clues and guidance are you noticing? Have you seen the same thing time and time again, and thought, 'Is someone trying to tell me something'?

b) Have you wondered whom to contact for help, and suddenly there's an advert, and then a friend also recommends them?

c) Have you dreaded the hurt that you may feel if you make certain changes, but that feeling in your stomach strengthens you, and makes it clear that you must take that important first step?

d) Have you woken up in the morning with a defined idea of something you must do?

e) Have you passed a homeless person sitting on the pavement, and later wished you'd followed your gut feeling and got them a sandwich?

f) Have you felt guilty putting recyclable waste in with the rubbish, and later wished you'd made the effort to do it properly?

g) Have you wondered how you could get involved in something you've never done before like spiritual meetings, meditation, environmental or charity work, astronomy, astrology, Reiki etc., and then you met someone, who offered to take you?

h) Have you sat and worked out all the complicated ways to do something, and then suddenly wham, there in your mind is a very simple way that's so obvious?

i) Have you ever found that you have the right answers to things that you didn't know you knew?

j) Have you had a significant word or name in your mind leading you to get in touch with someone, or act on the meaning of the word?

These are all clues in life's treasure hunt. But for it to work, you must act on it, because the flow of information will then become stronger. We receive many guiding messages, but so often we ignore them. It reminds me of the film, Bruce Almighty, which I think illustrates it brilliantly. It shows the main character played by Jim Carrey driving along a highway and getting mad at God. He demands that He sends him a sign. Meanwhile he ignores road signs telling him to be cautious, and slow down. But he's so incensed that he's blind to them all and crashes the car, which he then also blames on God.

There are times where you expect a sign like a bolt of lightning or a burning bush, and what do you get? A directory falling open or a feeling in your stomach that you need to do something.

Guidance may simply be *a flash of inspiration!* Just learn to follow it and make life simple for yourself. As God sees you reacting positively to your guidance, He will help you to find other positive ways of communicating more. You won't always get things right, but don't beat yourself up when that happens. Every day you're learning.

Personally Speaking, I've found that making some choices can be hard. When I chose to train as a spiritual healer, I had to choose between two courses. I liked both but preferred one in particular; but was it the right one? The more I thought about it, the more I confused myself! So, when I went to bed one night, I asked for guidance. 'Which course should I choose please, God?'

When I woke the following morning I knew exactly which one I needed to go on, and I knew it had been a guided choice, because it wasn't the one I thought I preferred. But it proved to be the right course, and a year later I was qualified.

Anyway, I was satisfied that the choice carried God's approval, so that was good enough for me. My first Spirit Guide, White Cloud then told me that although I was blessed as a healer that wouldn't be my main focus in my work. He was right.

Yes, I could have gone with the other course, but what would it have gained me? I have always found that following your guidance takes you where you **need** to be.

Seeing My Guidance

When we close our eyes, we may see people, scenes or even colours. Some of what we see may make sense, and some may not, but if you want to strengthen that link, you can visit a Spiritualist Centre and ask about their development courses. It's an option that you can build on or ignore. But always ensure that you develop with qualified people.

Speaking Personally, When I first tried to communicate, I was searching for the best way for me. Twice I heard a distinct voice in my head, but this didn't develop. Instead, while I was training as a spiritual healer, I attended other workshops too that could develop my awareness and help me recognise spirit communication.

At one, a group of us sat in a circle, and we were each paired off with someone we didn't know. We weren't allowed to ask our partner anything, but we had to discover some details about them. So, we all relaxed and did our best to link. We were warned not to change any details.

When I closed my eyes and relaxed, I saw a beautiful blue eye. Just one. Of course, my mind started to interfere, and I decided that maybe there was a connection between this woman and a blonde person with blue eyes. Well, I couldn't just say I saw a blue eye, *could I?*

My turn came. I built up my courage and said, 'I saw a blue eye'. The instructor turned to the woman and asked, 'Are you a healer?' to which she replied 'Yes'.

That day I learned 3 valuable lessons!
1. I could use that sense of communication.
2. I needed to be accurate with my information.

3. A blue eye is the symbol for a healer.

I didn't often receive my messages that way, But I remember one night being shown a satin shroud. The following morning, I learned of the death of Princess Diana.

It was about a year later that I found that I could also channel information, and that has been my main connection ever since.

We can receive communication in different ways, and you'll get to know what works for you.

But I do emphasise that not everyone wants or needs to develop these advanced skills of clairsenscience, clairaudience, or clairvoyance, so don't feel pressured into doing so.

Receiving simple instinctive guidance and then acting on your gut feeling are powerful enough for most people's life journeys. And that allows you to live a full life while you follow your most powerful route.

An Exercise In Forgiving

Forgiveness is for many people, what Becher's Brook is to horses, when they run the Grand National at Aintree Racecourse. It's the place where they're most likely to fall.

You may know the theory of forgiving; but when you're emotionally in pain, you may hold on to the hurt and even build on it. You may think it's unnatural to forgive those who inflicted the pain, but if you hold on to their rubbish, that will only sour *your* life.

Those who caused the hurt, do have to pay, whether here or in the Spirit Realms. And if you've heard of Karma, you'll understand when I say that what goes around really does come around!

So, forgive them, mentally and spiritually and release yourself from their rubbish. People must learn from their mistakes, but you don't have to be a part of it anymore.

When You Create the Pain

How many times have you said, 'I can't forgive myself for doing that'?

Well, you won't free yourself to move on unless you ask God for forgiveness and also forgive yourself.

Yes, you're a sinner! We all are! But a large part of your learning comes from making the wrong decisions. The more serious they are, the greater the payback is. The important thing is that you recognise your wrongs and use that understanding in a positive way. Simply ask forgiveness and forgive yourself, because when you don't, it's a barrier to your future.

Why Is Forgiveness So Important?

If you forgive mistakes, you take what you can from the hurtful lesson and move on. That means that you free off your life to take on new and better experiences. A negative situation has the value of providing greater understanding, so let go of the rubbish and free yourself.

Forgiveness de-clutters the mind, it heals you and it clears many of the barriers that would have otherwise impeded your future growth, your wellbeing and even your mental and physical health.

So how do you begin to switch off this persistent power of unforgiveness?

Forgiveness Exercise

Along with every other person on this planet, you have to accept that you won't always make the right decisions, for it's your own mistakes and those you endure from others that often provide your most potent lessons. So how do you set up a regular maintenance plan, in order to ensure that you're not building barriers to overcome on your own life path?

From time to time sit down and make a list of what you need to forgive. Include everything that you loathe and things that irritate you, and from which you need to move on. Remember to include your own faults too. Only you and God will see the list so be completely honest.

Hold the paper and read the list out loud if you can, otherwise silently to yourself, and then ask God to release you from it by using this Forgiveness Prayer.

I ask, Dear Heavenly Power, for a structure to be given that allows me to move forward in my life without the ardour of hate or unforgiveness.

Please take the names and issues from this paper and allow me the forgiveness that shall empower me to a new stage in my life, where I carry no malice, and feel worthwhile about myself and others.

I ask this in the knowing of God's love given. Amen.

Once you've said the prayer, destroy the paper in a shredder or fire. Allow yourself to feel free.

In Section 3 in Prayers, you'll find a Daily Forgiveness Prayer given to me by God. It's beautiful, so please share it.

Unconditional Love, A Natural Partner To Forgiveness

Be prepared to, without any conditions, love everyone in your day, each day. You may not like them but that's completely different.

You *can't* always like people who upset areas of your life or others' lives, but you can send them unconditional love to help them to learn and heal that darkness within them. You'll probably benefit from their better attitude.

Were they rude to you? Maybe they're having a bad day. Do they always behave badly towards you? Realise they may be less advanced than you on the spiritual learning curve, so forgive them, and ask God to help them to learn and become better people.

If you've suffered a big hurt in your life, forgive those responsible, because as I described earlier, they have to settle their own karma account, and by carrying your own hate, resentment, or loathing, you merely sabotage your own life, which is a waste of time and energy. Instead, send them your unconditional healing love. Love is something that you don't run out of when you use it. God keeps topping it up!

You're being bullied? Pray for the courage to do what's right and realise that the bullies can only win mentally if you let them.

You're bullying others? Maybe you don't realise you're intimidating people, maybe you do. Pray for forgiveness, and ask God to help you to love yourself, and behave in a kinder way, then you can use that power and determination within you to help people, and not bully them. It's ultimately more rewarding for your present life and beyond.

Get Your Mind, Body, And Spirit Primed For Take Off

Now you know the basis of why you're here, and you know that you'll receive help and guidance from God and His Team when you ask; but to achieve what you need from life as a whole, you should ensure that you're functioning at your optimum level. Major physical or mental issues may present extra challenges, but you can manoeuvre around many problems, and vitalise your life in a far more powerful way, when you work with God's help. You're an evolving being, and so you encounter change every day in some way; it's there to develop you and challenge you in whatever form is required, and you're surrounded by the energies you need on your journey.

How you react to that is up to you, but you must consider that negativity is a dead end, because it blinds you to the opportunities that may present themselves, and it may also make you deaf to the support offered by others. It's a 'no-brainer'. Stay positive!

Positivity can ***open*** up the options, because as you radiate positive energies you attract more back. Anyway, you should know by now that you have a lot going for you. You're not going to waste that, are you?

So, let's get to the nitty gritty bits......

Start to Heal and Balance Your System

To become the best version of you, you need to ensure that the whole of you is balanced to its optimum.

Deal with any nagging aches, pains, and other minor disorders. Don't just suffer them. Your self-esteem may be low because you simply don't allow the time to consider your own needs.

Your stress level may have risen because of other people's requirements, as well as your own, and this may have borne down on you enough that you've finally reached your elastic limit, the point where, you have to let go of some of those strains. If you fail to do that you may end up in a far worse situation where your health could really suffer.

So, it's time to prioritise because you don't want to lose your focus now. Some issues may be unsolvable in the long term, but you may still be able to improve some elements. Where possible, use natural remedies and therapies, because some medicines can also fog up your brain and your body when you take them.

You should always check with your doctor before you stop medicines or start certain supplements, but the side effects with some medication can make it worthwhile investigating the alternatives.

In the exercise 'Nourish Your Mind And Body' you'll explore your diet in more detail, and that's important, because it can help you to define the optimum foods that will fulfil you physically; and with patience and a little effort, you may trace and rectify less serious problems without medication, and the effect of that can energise your body and your mind.

Similarly, if you have an underweight or overweight issue, don't clutter up your brain by grumbling and feeling depressed about it. Instead take the first steps that help you to find the right solution. Once you do, you'll start feeling more in control.

Quality of food is also important. The fresher and better quality you buy, the more it'll fulfil your nutritional needs. As you answer those you'll find you become sharper mentally, and your physical health will be better. Try not to clutter your body with lots of rubbish food containing additives (which may also have side effects).

This is a time of action and not just thoughts, so if you feel a deep need to give up smoking or drinking, get help and do it. Apply that call to action in all areas of your clearing process, and you'll benefit greatly.

Day to day maintenance helps your overall wellbeing. It's that simple, after all, you maintain your car, your washing machine, and your computer! Well, this is far more important to you, so start maintaining your own mind, body, and soul! After all, one health subject alone highlights the importance of looking after yourself...... Cancer. We are told that one in every two of us will suffer cancer within our lifetime. It's frightening that for so many they no longer wonder if they'll be affected. They wonder when! So, let's turn the negativity into positive action, and begin looking at prevention. Here are some suggestions:

Running like Clockwork

Getting in tune, mentally, physically, and spiritually makes you a winner, because no matter what your goal is, you are, as far as possible, in complete balance. It may not be feasible to achieve 100%, but the closer you allow yourself to become, the greater the benefit will be. Every part of you was designed to work together, so your efforts to be better balanced, or your lack of them, will show.

- Mind – Remove yourself from any unnecessary stresses and address the necessary ones.

- Body – Make changes in diet or exercise gradually. Don't make random cuts in your diet, or over exercise your body if you're not used to it.
- Spirit / Soul – Don't separate off the spiritual part from your practical day and then escape to it when everything goes pear shaped. Incorporate it in the whole. It belongs there and will help you to feel better.

Achieve Optimum Balance

Maybe in the past you've not expected to change much. In past generations it wasn't unusual for a man to reach retirement age in the same employment he joined after leaving school, and women mainly left their jobs to have a family and care for them. Life followed a very traditional pattern because that was expected. But that doesn't apply now in most families. We're breaking down that barrier.

So, if you've felt that life was like a straightjacket that you couldn't wriggle out of, it's no longer the case, and when you draw in the spiritual needs of your journey, God's Team will guide and empower you so that you focus on what's needed. But remember this is your life and God will ensure you live it according to your choices because you have free will. So don't expect God to change this and that. Don't blame God for not making things easy for you. They weren't meant to be. But do ask for the help to help yourself.

I can tell you now that you can master amazing things, even if you're not physically able to do everything.

You're the star of this show! So, no matter where you are now, with a positive outlook from you, together with the empowerment and support you'll find from working with God and His Team, you're already on your way.

You've started creating a working life structure. Just as important now is to achieve and maintain a healthy balance within your life, and we'll cover areas of that within this section.

The structure of your whole being needs to be as well balanced as possible, so when it comes to your overall viability there's a lot to cover. Once you do the initial checks, it's then up to you to maintain your optimum mind, body, and spirit health, because it's precious to your journey. This doesn't exclude you if you're disabled, it's simply a matter of achieving your best within those parameters.

To begin with, is your life panning out as you intended?

How much of *'you'* do you recognise, or have you conformed so much to other people's advice and influence that you're no longer sure? Has your passion for life been replaced by a need for a higher financial status? Or do you manage to balance that with your soul's challenges?

- Are you the one that yearned to follow a different career, but got persuaded out of it?
- Are you the one that feels imprisoned by circumstances, and can't see a way out?
- Are you the one who feels passionate about certain issues in the world, but lacks the courage to get involved?
- Are you the one who ended up different to others, because a part of your brain or physical body doesn't work properly?
- Are you the one who has failed so many times, that you now believe nothing will work?
- Are you the one who feels that you're too old now? That it's too late?

- Are you the one who bottomed out in life and can't see the way up?
- Are you the one who's somewhere you don't want to be, but don't know how to change direction? Or……
- Are you the one who got it right, because you felt the passion for life, and followed it through?

It's easy to say, 'Well this is where life led me', but how much resistance did you put up? If you follow blindly in someone else's shadow, you won't experience the deep-down joy that you can achieve walking your own path in the sun.

There may be many reasons why you end up in a different place to where you needed or even wanted, so there's an unchallenged part in most people, and if that applies to you, life will remain unfulfilling until you change your focus.

Speaking Personally, I learned many things in my early life, but I couldn't recognise my real power until I began walking my own path years later. Everything then began to resonate with me, but I still had to receive the guidance and empowerment from God to hone my direction. Looking back, I know my lessons were chosen by others and I didn't feel strong enough to change that. I didn't want to upset other people's lives, so I was not in control of my own. Fortunately, when I married I had the support and love of my husband Mike and 47 years later he's still there. Life has taught me though that we must pay attention to all our lessons, because then we can understand ourselves and others better.

Nourish Your Mind And Body

It may seem strange talking about your diet as part of your spiritual programme, but what you consume can affect your physical and mental health, and it's an area where you can help yourself so start taking charge.

Spiritually you can benefit because when you feel good, you have a buzz, and your energies are high. Whereas, when you feel low, your zest and energy as a whole suffer, and this can have an impact on every part of your life.

Reaching for pills and powders may show that there's something wrong, but they don't deal with the root cause. So, heed your mind and body needs and let's start looking at prevention instead.

With so much food affected by artificial additives, preservatives, crop pesticides, genetic modification and forced farming, you have to be aware that you're eating the results. It's not just the immediate effects, there can also be a gradual accumulation of chemicals growing within you because of the toxins absorbed in so many ways by your body.

By using your awareness and resolving to take a hand in assessing your own health issues, you can often improve the way you feel, your alertness, and your long-term body, mind, and soul health. It's also a subject that may inspire you to support those who fight for a healthier environment, because, like animals we might also be ingesting plastics.

You may rely on your body and mind being healthy, and yet if they give you no problems, or you accept certain changes as a result of age or lifestyle, you may at some point experience a painful nudge.

So, check your dietary needs from time to time.

You can do this by dowsing with a pendulum, but if you don't know how, then use a set of playing cards. You're looking for a simple YES or NO to specific questions. The guiding energies around you enable you to do this, and the answers can be very clear.

If you're using cards then remove the Joker. No one's joking here.

1. Decide the colour for 'YES'. Let's say for this exercise that red is 'Yes' and black is 'NO'.
2. Hold the cards and ask God to bless them.
3. Shuffle them.

Have a notepad handy so that you can take notes, and then, most important of all……. Act on the information. Remember, no action, no change!

First question to ask:

1. Is my diet suitable for me?

Pick a card. Is it red or black? If it's red there's nothing more to ask, because that's telling you that your diet is fine. But if it's a black suit that is telling you that you need to change your diet a little.

Put the card in the middle of the deck and go to the next question.

2. Should my optimum diet include -
- Meat?
- Fish?
- Seafood?

Make a note of each answer, and if they were: YES (red), move straight to question 4, but if one or two are NO, you should consider omitting those foods. If they were all NO (black), then go first to question 3:

3. Do I need a diet that is –
Vegetarian?
Vegan?
Raw Food?

Continue the same process for all the questions.

4. Do I need an Alternative Diet such as –
- Gluten Free?
- Lactose Free?
- Wheat Free?
- An Exclusion diet to source Food Allergy or Intolerances?
- A more Alkaline Diet?

- Caffeine Free?
- Dairy Free?
- Egg Free?
- Casein Free?
- Kosher?
- Organic?
- Soya Free?
- Yeast Free?
- Suitable for Diabetics?

There are also questions you can ask when you suspect a dietary problem. For example:

5. Do I have an intolerance to nuts?

6. Do I have an allergy to nuts?

If the answer is Yes, then go through the various types of nuts and check them. It may not be that you have a problem with all nuts, so check the different types.

7. Do I drink enough water? This is an important question.

8. Do I react to certain E labels? If so, check which ones.

Lastly, ask this question:

9. Do I need to take supplements?

If the answer is Yes, go to a complete list of vitamins and minerals such as www.simple-approach-to-healthy-living.com and check there.

There's a lot of investigation work that you can do for yourself, in order to help fulfil your mind and body needs, and armed with ideas, you can then make changes.

Alternatively, contact a professional nutritionist, who will test you.

Finally, remember to monitor your mind and body needs regularly. The results won't always stay the same. Imbalances can occur and when they do, you'll not be on your best form, so that's the time to check again whether you need to make any changes.

Explore The Natural Power Of Colour

One of the background tools that God has given humanity is an awareness of colour. It's everywhere, and it's empowering and yet you may not realise the positive effect it can have on your daily life.

Colour is a basic part of your aura, the energy field that surrounds you. There are many colours within it, but unless your eyes are accustomed to auras, you may only see them as a white energy.

An example is in the photograph of Di Wall's aura. She's a powerful reader and Counsellor for Cartouche, and her aura clearly shows the spirit support she receives with two clear images of a Pharaoh within her auric energy. She was attending one of our retreats at the time.

Colour fills the natural world around you, and you can feed off through crystals, it can also heal you.

While some may make you feel particularly good, others may not give you the same buzz. That's your senses working and guiding you to the colours that can boost your aura and your inner system.

Colour Choices – An Inspiration or Not

Many developed countries have their own logical and traditional vision of power dressing, and yet, it can often paint a sombre picture of grey, brown, and black.

In contrast, the colours worn in many poorer countries are vibrant, because the people naturally pick those that can help raise their spirits to face any challenging days.

So, where possible, be guided by colour. Not all meetings need you to power dress. Wear the colours that inspire you for those important occasions. In that way you'll be empowering yourself.

Surround yourself with the colours that lift your mood. Flowers, upholstery, cushions, and pictures can change the energy in a room.

God has been generous with shades and tones to light up your day. Let them inspire you. Bright or subtle, they all do a job. So don't be colour blind.

The Healing Countryside

The Spring colours of the woodlands bring fresh new life, and the subtle reds, yellows, and browns tone the shortening days of Autumn. A walk through a forest can clear the stagnancy of the past and awaken your energies to new beginnings.

It can be the most therapeutic exercise you can take as you 'breathe' in the vibrant colours of each season. Stand with your back against a tree or sit on a bench and simply absorb the rich energies of your surroundings. Also, if the sea is close or there's a river nearby, you can relax with the gentle sounds of moving water. Your senses can serve you well when you allow them, and it's all healing.

See and Eat Colour

To nourish our inner needs, we add the dynamism of spices, fresh vegetables, and fruit.

What could be better than building a rainbow of colours on your dinner plate from the many natural foods available to you. It can strike a wonderful balance on which you can feast your eyes and gain a nutritionally rich diet.

So be aware of colour because it's such an important energy, and to ignore it is to waste a valuable and enjoyable aid to life.

Living with Colour

In your own surroundings, give some thought to the colours around you at home. Let them soothe you, energise you, inspire you, and even send you to sleep!

Alert yourself to a need for the right colours at work too. If options are limited, then find a way to have a small splash of vibrant or soothing shades that you can focus on now and then, or walk home through your local park, or the flower section of a supermarket and soak up those energies!

Power Dress Your Day

God could have created a black and white world, but the colours He brought have a purpose. It's an important range of energies that He has made available to everyone. Some can comfort you, or help you to feel vibrant and confident, while others calm you, and lift your spirits. Be aware of this and get to know the colours that empower you, in your wardrobe choices.

For example, red is a great colour for power dressing, but choose the shade that you feel right in. Red focuses on the colour of your base chakra, which relates to a feeling of security and power. But it has to be the shade, which makes you feel good and energised.

Colour coordination may guide you to a fashionable winter, spring, summer, and autumn collection that enhances your natural colouring, but don't be afraid to wear shades that empower you as they have an even greater value. When you feel good in a colour, you glow naturally.

If you're able to wear your own clothes, rather than a uniform in your working day, then introduce colours that make you feel good. They'll inspire your day. Try to surround yourself with the ones that excite your senses, energise you and possibly make your stomach leap. It will make you feel so much better. Colour is a generous gift from God so don't discount it. When you pick right, you'll notice the difference and so will everyone else.

Crystals

Just like colour, crystals can energise, heal, and generally lighten up your day, and it's worth going to a holistically informed crystal seller to be guided to the ones appropriate to your needs. However, at the same time you should use your own awareness to choose your particular stone.

The experts can guide you on the sort of crystal you need if you have a specific problem, but there's a common saying with crystal experts, 'the stone chooses you'. So, learn to recognise the crystals that attract you, and then pick the one that calls out to you. It may not be the brightest, largest, or prettiest, but it's the stone that's telling you 'pick me, I'm the right energy for you'.

Hold it in your hand for a minute. You may feel a buzz of energy. Don't worry if you don't.

Take the stone home and cleanse it because it's been touched and held by many people, and it still carries their energies. Rinse it under the tap and feel you're washing them away. Then let it absorb yours. Hold it and programme it by asking it to help you in the way you need, then carry it within your aura in a pocket or underwear. Sleep with it under your pillow.

It's fine to show other people your crystal, but don't hand it around because it will gather their energies and you've programmed it to specifically work with yours.

Because your crystal is working all the time, you should recharge it regularly because the process is depleting its healing properties. To enable it to charge, place the stone weekly in a sunny or light position on a windowsill for a few hours to recover, alternatively let it sit in the gentler energies of the moonlight.

Crystals are loyal friends and a fascinating subject, so why not get a book on them to help you understand more.

Declutter Your Life

We're a race of collectors, and so much of what we gather stays with us until we actually decide, 'This is rubbish' or that 'It's no longer of benefit to me'. That may be so in our physical lives but it's also true in that storage bin called, 'The Mind'. Mostly it's memories coloured by failure, rejection, misunderstanding and other various types of stress.

Clear Mental Clutter

The In Tray for your mind fills daily with any negative experiences, and together with fears and phobias they can all create a feeling of inadequacy.

Add the clutter that surrounds you physically, such as jobs you haven't yet finished, those you haven't started, and the help you offered but never fulfilled, and suddenly your brain adopts a position of stagnant failure.

A cluttered mind becomes negative, and your expectation for the future can drain away, so if you reach the point where your mind is muddled and you don't know the way out, then start by forgiving yourself.

A Prayer for Self-Forgiveness (Use this each day until your mind is free)

I ask Dear Heavenly Power to be forgiven for my actions and inactions, and any hurt brought. Allow me the peace of knowing that I am forgiven and help me to forgive; for the strength and power that is given by God shall enable me to then move on. Amen.

Simplify Your Life

Make a list of tasks you must complete and prioritise it so that more urgent ones are at the top. Then, one by one work through them. Don't avoid or delay awkward ones because you need them finished and out of your mind. I can assure you that afterwards you'll feel so much freer.

From that point on, keep on top of the jobs that need doing, and it'll lift your mood so that you feel good about yourself.

By making life simpler, you approach the day in a more organised way and your life will run smoothly and efficiently. You'll not remove the positive energies of sentiment and love from your day; you'll simply make more space for them. By clearing the rubbish, and catching up on jobs and commitments, you're allowing yourself space for the important things that need your loving attention. That way you're giving your life the best version of you, and that allows you to achieve more.

It's tempting to say, 'I'll do it tomorrow', but that won't set you free to focus on the more important issues. Be organised. You may wonder what this has to do with spirituality, but it's an important step towards working in balance, and when that happens you achieve more, because you're in tune with the energies around you.

Clear Soul Clutter

It may sound strange to say 'Declutter your soul' but it's a worthwhile thing to do.

Some problems in this life may have come from negative experiences in a past one. If ignored, they can have an overriding effect on your general progress and development.

Problems come from being either the victim or the perpetrator. Both lessons are there for you at some point on your journey, and if you still carry the negative energy from past lives, you may be repeating the same stifling or even destructive pattern in this one, because those experiences haven't been cleared by a process of regression and forgiveness. Look for a Regression and Release therapist to clear the problems but ensure they are recommended or qualified to help you.

If you feel that there's something overriding you in your life and possibly making you feel depressed, it's possible that you have a Spirit Attachment. They're spirits that have remained within the Earth Plane, rather than going to the Spirit Realms.

If that is the case, search online for Spirit Release. There are associations that list therapists. They should also manage to deal with curses.

For a demonic influence seek the help of an ordained minister. There are organisations that will guide you on all these problems.

If the therapists don't include forgiveness in their procedure, then remember to do so afterwards in order to sever the effect of the problems.

If you struggle to find therapists then talk to your nearest Spiritualist Church or Centre. They'll be able to guide you.

Clear the Clutter Around You

If you're someone who stores unused items in the loft, or your home is cluttered with things you've forgotten you had, then pass them on to someone who can use them. The same within your car or shed, avoid accumulating items that are no use to you, but don't waste them, there are charities and up cyclers who may be glad of them.

Make Life Simpler

Without intending to, we can all fall into a habit of untruths.

The more truthful you are in your life, the more it frees your power, and you earn others' trust. It also removes the complications that come with lies and fibs, untangling the knots and helping your energies to flow more freely.

When you pray, you always need to be sincere, but what about those little white lies that slip into conversations, together with excuses that trip off your tongue when you let someone down. It may be a process of self-protection but you're better than that, and the little white lie you told lessens your true power.

Honesty counts, so be gentle but truthful. 'I'm sorry, I forgot' works far better than, 'Well it's like this' ….. and a neatly woven story.

When you lie, God knows, you know and probably the person you're talking to knows! So, live in truth.

The Power of Contemplation

It's so much easier to recognise help and guidance when you're relaxed. You'll find that communication is easier and suddenly you're open for business. So don't stress and confuse yourself.

When you have a few minutes available, relax with, or without, some gentle music, and in that way you can allow yourself to be available for any guiding feelings.

Meditate or gently contemplate and your senses will then have the space to help you to develop.

Spiritual groups can help you to develop your awareness. If that's the route you take, feel relaxed and it'll happen.

If you're finding a quiet moment at home, keep a notebook handy and jot down the various thoughts and inspirational ideas that waft through your relaxed mind. It can be an inspiring guide to new things. You may see colours when you close your eyes, and these may be healing you. Maybe it's a tune, that will link you to a special memory, or the words will be significant to you.

Personally Speaking, I used to walk a lot in the Derbyshire countryside. Ambling down quiet roads, I would often be given the Carpenters' song 'I'm on top of the world looking down on creation' and I'd thank my spirit team for being there with me.

I remember finishing a day's work at a Mind Body Spirit Fair in the UK, where I'd been bringing channelled guidance to clients, and I asked God if I had done a good enough job. I was immediately given The Hallelujah

Chorus from Handel's Messiah! It made me smile. Certain tunes have been there as a response in my head at such appropriate moments! It's a matter of getting used to spirit's different ways of communicating. Allow them and they can make life more fun.

When you do relax, the fog of everyday confusion can clear, and it opens the doors for God's Team to help you tune in on their guidance.

De-Stress
With Prayer

Assess what it is that makes you stressed. If it's a combination of things then, make a list and separate what's necessary from the unnecessary. Do what you have to in order to shed the excess. Relax and talk to God about the area(s) left. Chat to Him about it or use this prayer:

'I am ready now, Dear Heavenly Power to structure my life differently and I want the effectiveness to reach through to my own need to release stress.

I realise that stress is inevitable in some situations, however I've reached a point, where it's limiting my capacity because I get no break from the ramblings of a mind that never sleeps. Let me now take forward my life in a different, less distorted way that allows me to shine and feel equipped for my path ahead. I ask this of God in whom I trust. Amen.'

Don't be afraid to use this stress releasing prayer any time. You won't overdose and God won't get fed up with you.

Forms of Relaxing: Other ways of dealing with stress in your life are:
- Relaxation exercises
- Yoga
- A walk in the country
- A walk in the park or by the river if you're in a town.

- Meditation
- Listening to relaxing music

Two Earth Exercises To Relax And Revitalise

It's so easy to become swallowed up by your day, and yet if you find a few minutes for yourself, it'll benefit you mentally, physically, and emotionally. Impossible? No, it isn't! You just *have* to make room for yourself. The elves would call it 'working smarter', and they know a thing or two about that!

So, find some relaxation space or a diversion from your normal working timetable, and at the same time, plan in one or both of these exercises.

Both use the Earth's energies, which are very powerful, so welcome to another energy source you may not have recognised before now.

The first exercise is particularly good if you've been rushing around and are a bit stressed:

How to Calm Your Pulse

This first simple exercise is one that you can do anywhere. We can overlook the Earth's power, and yet it has a valuable energy.

Allow yourself three or four minutes for the exercise. If you're sitting in the car waiting to go to an important appointment like a job interview, just as a safety precaution lock the doors because you'll have your eyes closed. So, Let's begin.

1. First of all, relax your body by finding somewhere comfortable, adjust any cushions and close your eyes.
2. Visualise your feet throwing out roots and securing themselves to the ground (even if you're in the car).
3. Now, focus on the base of your spine. Let your mind go to that place where you daydream, and then form a mental picture of the lower end of

your spine. If you can't, don't worry, not everyone can. Instead, just imagine the letter **L** as the point where, while you're sat down, your spine meets your hips and legs. That is the base you're focusing on. See it in your mind.
4. Take a breath and calmly say these words, **'I ask the Earth to harmonise my heartbeat with the Earth's energies'**.
5. Repeat the sentence once more.
6. As you sit there, your pulse will soon lower, and you'll feel calm.

    Once complete, with your eyes closed, mentally clingwrap yourself fully in God's White Light, and thank Him and the Earth. Open your eyes and then get on with your day.

Personally Speaking, I've Seen This Work. My husband was due for one of his diabetes checks with the consultant, but the hospital car park was small and parking places had been snapped up. We'd asked the angels for help and at about three minutes before the appointment, a car moved out and we moved in. We dashed to the waiting room, hassled and out of breath! Mike sat quietly and did the Earth exercise. As he finished the nurse arrived, 'We'll do your checks, Michael.' Off they went. A few minutes later, he came back smiling, 'Pulse and blood pressure fine', he said.

Obviously, if you have a condition that doesn't allow your pulse to calm, it won't show you a false reading, because that would be counteractive to you getting help. But if your health is basically good, this short exercise can be useful.

Revitalise your Energy Field

This second exercise is a visualisation one to do when you feel your energies are a bit low, and you've lost that buzz.

1. Begin by settling yourself into a comfy chair, and ensure your feet are on the floor. Imagine that they're throwing out roots into the ground, so you feel secure and comfortable.
2. Close your eyes and take yourself to that relaxed and welcoming part of your mind, the place of daydreams. Once you're there, simply visualise a small 'tap' in the sole of your left foot.
3. Mentally, turn it on and visualise the stale energy draining from your body and falling deep down into the Earth, where it'll be revitalised.
4. Now you need to mentally turn on the small 'tap' in the sole of your right foot, where a golden glowing energy is now being drawn from the Earth and starting its journey.
5. First, it'll fill your right foot before climbing gradually up your leg into the right side of your body.
6. Slowly it'll spread up your right side, replacing the old, tired energies and refreshing each part of you as it goes.
7. As the golden energy reaches your shoulders it'll flow down your right arm, all the way down to your fingertips. Feel a tingle as you stretch them.
8. The flow of golden light then rises up through your neck and into your head, filling it with this beautiful glowing energy, allowing its power to penetrate your brain, as well as all those taut muscles in your face and neck.
9. It'll then begin its flow back down through your neck and into the left side of your body, refreshing the stiff muscles in your shoulder before filling your left arm and hand with the Earth's loving energy. Stretch your fingers so that it reaches the tips.
10. This beautiful force will then travel down the left side of your body, the vibrant energy gradually

filling it and then flowing down your left leg, pushing the remaining old energies lower and lower on their journey to the Earth.
11. As this amber energy reaches your toes it's almost completed its course. Once your foot fills with the gold, you need to mentally turn off both taps.
12. You are now glowing with this beautiful energising force from the Earth. Bathe in the glow of this energy for a few minutes.
13. Clingwrap yourself in God's White Light, thank Him and the Earth, open your eyes, and then resume your day, refreshed.

Become You

You may be shouting out *'but I am me'*! However, with so many influences and distractions around you, your true passion for life may have waned. So, it's time to focus on the elements within each day that hold you back.

William Shakespeare said, 'All the world's a stage and all the men and women merely players. They have their exits and their entrances.' But are you wasting your time acting out someone else's role when you should be focusing on your own?

In your life you may learn many ways to help you to progress forward in the way civilised man demands. Some are essential to your spiritual journey, but others may not fit the blueprint that you helped God design for you.

So, when I say, 'Be you' it may sound elementary and straightforward, but when you consider all the teaching, coercion, and well-meaning guidance /pressure that you experience in life, the 'real you' can easily get lost.

Just as a shiny new coin gathers flaws as soon as it gets handled, your life may also carry a few impressions from others' influences.

- It's already affected by the strengths and weaknesses you inherited mentally and physically from your parents and their families.
- As a baby within the womb, you were aware of any stresses and upsets that affected your mother during her pregnancy. These energies can promote guilt, a fear of being born, or even hostility, as unsurprisingly the unborn child feels the emotion of its parent.
- You may have had a traumatic birth.
- You may be carrying influences from a past life, which then become more evident when you're an adult.

It's true to say that many influences are there for you very early in life. As you grow, you're guided by adults around you, and you live by their code. Certain elements help us to become considerate and loving human beings. Those are positive influences that you need to nurture. The ones you need to consider changing are those that point you towards a different direction to your inner choices, those you feel passionate about, those that you instinctively feel you need to follow. They are from your soul.

Remember that just as that coin gathers energies from everyone who handles it, many people may have a hand on your life, confident that they know better than you. Some may have encouraged you to be the best version of you, but others will have brought a more restrictive vision to your life.

Consider these examples:

Despite how much you love, respect and may want to please your parents, and other family members, you may have adopted some of their opinions and tendencies, which don't sit right with you.

However, this is your life, not theirs. Take ownership of it and your beliefs.

Certain teachers may have influenced you in ways that no longer apply to your current life.

However, personal freedom is yours, and your generation needs to move on with the best of decisions. It's never too late to change.

Did you take up a career that wasn't your choice because you wanted to be loyal or please someone other than yourself?

Ideally: You must be comfortable in your job to give of your best. Why work at something in a mediocre way because your heart's not in it, when you can do what you really need to do with passion?

Do you follow certain values because of peer pressure?

Should you really make choices that you're not comfortable with?

Society or some authority may have influenced you in a way that doesn't make you feel good about yourself.

But you could break out and show your true colours. You may end up leading rather than following.

Advertisers may attempt to persuade you to want what they want to sell, but do you really need it or desire it?

Common sense says that you shouldn't allow yourself to be influenced by them if you don't agree. Instead, you could become an influencer.

Maybe you get swallowed up by the need to earn more money but don't feel rewarded by life.

So, is it worth sacrificing personal reward for a financial one? Why not find a compromise that allows you to cover monetary needs while you develop an alternative route.

Maybe you struggle to keep up with the highflyers but question the mental and physical stress it puts you through.

Well then, it's time to be honest with yourself when it affects your health and relationships. What is life really worth to you?

Your life may have become weighted down by directions, outlooks, and obligations that don't fit your personal mould, and once you recognise that, you can begin to unravel and discard those things that are no longer valid to your direction, because you don't want to inhibit your progress. You may be keen to learn new things, but there are also those occasions where you first need to unlearn habits and outlooks taught by others to make way for those that sit well with the new you.

You see, all the time you're carrying others' influences that don't fit you, you're allowing them to conceal the 'Real You'. So, work with the truth, and you'll progress faster, your life will become sincere and true to *your* needs, and the end result will be that each day will be much more rewarding.

People around you may not be happy that you are making that move, and they may even try to dissuade you. So be prepared. If you move away from the pressures of some social circles because they no longer satisfy your needs, others will soon replace them as you become the person you *need* to be.

Remember that you count. You're unique so celebrate it, and don't try to hide it!

Act out *your* role in life, and not that shaped by those who don't know the real you. Your life will flow better, make you feel good, and you'll achieve more with less stress.

So, monitor what you're doing, and whether it benefits your life. You may act out of habit and not even notice shortcomings. Whereas when you become the real **You,** you recognise better your strengths and weaknesses, and you forgive the mistakes you've made. You should understand that God isn't expecting a superhuman. He knows that it's inevitable that you'll make mistakes, and that when used properly even failures have made you stronger, more tolerant, and more humble. A better version of you.

Care For Your Soul
Flexing Your Soul's Muscles

Your soul needs nourishing as much as your mind and body. Ask most people and they would agree that as well as being enjoyable, food provides necessary nutrients for the body, similarly, some people also realise the benefit of feeding their mind, but only a few understand the value of nourishing their soul, and yet that's essential for your journey ahead.

To briefly recap, when you were still simply a soul within the Spirit Realms, you appreciated that to develop you had to face certain challenges on Earth, and that would be through specific experiences.

You were the one who decided what would enhance your learning at this stage of your eternal journey. God then generated the formula that became the human version of you and built the framework in which your life could develop. But it didn't stop there, because God also provided the support system that's there throughout your life. So how does that affect your soul?

Well, both the power within you and the amazing Power given to you by God and His Team are there to help your soul achieve what's necessary to aid its growth. When you develop, you gain in worth and this happens as a natural result of you fulfilling various goals through life, and how you appreciate it.

Your expectation within life grows as you see what's possible, and your abilities grow as you flex your soul's muscles and take the direction that helps you to achieve, not just for you, but for others too.

Going back to that word 'worth', let me explain it. Consider a basic building that's wind and watertight. It provides shelter and has a certain value.

But when you add electricity, and plumbing to the fabric of the building, you enhance its value. It's suddenly worth more to you, and offers more, not just in a monetary way. Similarly, you are building on your worth as you progress along your own positive pathway, and that happens as you develop goodness. You may see that as becoming more worthwhile.

It may be through the love you give to those around you, the caring actions you take, whether they be a love that's returned or unconditional love; and fulfilment comes from simple things like the joy you feel when you help others, or the way you cherish people, animals, life itself and the world around you. It makes you feel good when you share that, and it makes things better, helping you appreciate those parts of your life where you're growing.

Soul growth also comes from good and bad experiences that you live through, where you've faced up to the challenges, released the pain of the bad ones through forgiveness, and allowed yourself to grow from the lessons learnt.

These are challenges that you don't face alone because God is always there to help you, but there may be times when you pray for a bad situation to be taken away and this doesn't happen. That doesn't mean that God's deserted you, it simply happens that way, because it's an experience you singled out in your 'pre life' choices, and you ***have to*** go through with it, therefore God cannot break His contract with you and take it away. However, He's still there to help you through any difficulties and won't leave you. So, remain alert to all types of His guidance and support, and don't forget to talk to Him about how you feel.

In contrast to your life challenges and the reward they bring, there are life bonuses like a new sofa, car, and an expensive lifestyle. But these are just like fast food to your soul, and a diet of that alone would leave it undernourished, so enjoy treats but don't worship them!

They're acceptable for what they are, but to raise the value of them too high in your life, and ignore the needs of others, is to live an unbalanced life. Money is a tool and not a god. There's no soul nutrition in material things, and this is where a lot of people neglect their spiritual health in these times, because they're pursuing the wrong values.

There's nothing wrong with having some luxuries, but when you lose sight of the real meaning of your life, you also deprive it, because you'll be searching too much for what you can buy in the shopping centre and too little on the other priceless qualities that will develop you as a person.

Many successful people will freely admit that something is lacking in their lives. But they've become so wrapped up in the gruelling pursuit of material benefits in order to keep up with, or ahead of their peers that they can't identify what's lacking. But the odds are that spiritual satisfaction is certainly the supplement they need.

With your body's health, you have doctors and nutritionists to identify if your fat intake is too high or you're deficient in iron. But no one puts into simple terms what's lacking in your soul's diet. So, I hope this helps to clarify the importance of achieving your goals and nurturing your soul with positive development. Boost your life with God and He will help you to keep a better balance throughout, and then your main fulfilment will be earned with or without money.

Every person is made up of a mind, a body, and a spirit/soul. While the first two will wither and die, the soul is the part of you that will survive death and move on to the Spirit Realms and future lives, so nourish it for the next part of its journey both in this life and after.

Enrich Your Soul through Experience

Growth isn't guaranteed to be enjoyable. You'll also grow from enduring tragedy, poor health, or a disability. But then they are clear examples of when God can help empower you to cope with the hardship of what you are experiencing.

In contrast, you may have chosen to live a less demanding life this time, and that may be punctuated by some less severe challenges. Every life is different, but its map is accurate according to God's planning.

So how do you ensure that you lead your life to full advantage?

Look after your body. Care for it. It's the only casing you have and once it's worn out, apart from a few spare parts that you can replace along the way, you can't trade it in for a new one.

Live with a mind that's open to learning. You don't have to go to university to do this. Life is learning. You gain understanding from your interaction with people and from experiences, and you can use the knowledge you gain to help nourish your spirit, for when you put it to good purpose you're a winner, because you'll find fulfilment, and this is nectar to the soul. This is God rewarding your effort.

The more fulfilled you are, the more worthwhile you'll feel, and your soul will draw in the effect of it. Challenging yourself will grow your self-confidence. The knock-on effect is that others will also benefit, and this will increase your worth even more. Learning to grow from bad experiences will enhance your soul's growth, as will learning to forgive yourself and others, without resenting other people's seemingly comfortable lives. You must remember that things aren't always what they appear, and it's not for you to judge, because you won't see the whole picture. Accept this and it will bring harmony to your soul.

As you develop your understanding, you'll begin to look at what you have, rather than what you lack, and that then allows you to find a deeper fulfilment in your life, because it's in the direction that God needs for you.

Just as food that's full of additives is bad for your body, a life focused on the shallowness of material wealth isn't good for the soul, especially if it's achieved through debt. God encourages you to be debt free because it brings its own stress and upset which will act as a barrier to full soul health.

Make no mistake; wealth can be a great benefit, but only if it's used as a tool for yourself and to help in the world. When you do, you provide opportunity and growth. Money should be used with a purpose. You'll gain from the fulfilment it brings you, and your soul will be richer for it.

Be An Achiever

I ask you to commit yourself to a cause. Do it now!

Personally Speaking, it was early on in my work with Jesus when I learned the importance of helping others, because when you do, you help yourself too. Take it a step at a time, and then gradually expand what you're doing, because it will open up your life, and make you more aware. But where do you take that first step? Start to expect more from yourself. 'I can't' will become 'Where do I start?'

I was quickly plunged into the need to help others. I hadn't anticipated it so early on and I needed to respond. It wasn't that I didn't want to, but instead I wondered how my small efforts could ever make a difference, so Jesus guided me to directions that I hadn't considered, and with the inevitability of God's Power it then grew.

So, no more shrugged shoulders, and 'What can *I do?*' Instead, take a deep breath and ask in a positive way, '***What can I do?*** How do I start?' The answers will come, just wait.

It's amazing how the same words can bring very different emphasis. You move from helplessness to capability in one step, and the support will be there.

For me it started with helping offenders, then the homeless local to our home in Derbyshire, followed by taking aid out to Eastern Europe after the Balkans War. Your route may be quite different to mine, but the reward will be there.

Get Involved

We can lock ourselves away in our own environment, allowing ourselves enough of a glimpse of life that we're ready to make judgements. But take away the frequently sterile picture offered by TV and social media, dig deeper into what some people endure in life, and you may come away with a passion that asks, 'How can I stand by and do nothing? I must do something!' Just follow it and see where your guidance takes you.

There's charity work of different types locally, nationally, and internationally, but always check that your efforts are not just funding a glossy headquarters and high salaries. Ours was registered as Give Youth A Hand. It was small, volunteer run, our home was admin, aid warehouse and packing station, so we managed to keep our costs low. Not all organisations can manage that, but as a supporter you need to know that your contribution is helping the work you signed up for.

So, step out there, and enjoy what it brings you. It can be a very powerful journey.

Section 3:

Simply Life Changing Tools and Prayers

Simply Life Changing Tools Including: Bless Your Food; Honour Your Food; Protect Yourself; Love Unconditionally; Reawaken Your Instincts; Guidance And Healing Cards; Be Positively Powerful; Empower With Words; Let Others' Words Inspire You; Your Special Time; Be Tolerant; Heal Yourself; Use Kindness.

Tools to Relax You Including: Music; God's Love; Guided Meditation; Relax And Release Fatigue; The Five-Minute Refresher.

Prayers Including: What's In A Prayer; Speaking Personally; Put Together A Prayer; An Important Service of Clearance at the End of Your Life on Earth.

Personal Prayers Including: A Blessing For Your Food; Forgiveness; Personal Development; Self-Assurance; Coping With Personal Difficulties; Those Feeling Suicidal; Children; Healing; Natural Disasters; Peace; Terrorism; For The Injured; For The Souls Of Those Killed; The World and Planet Earth; Prayers For Animals; End Of Life Prayers For Animals.

Bless Your Food

By doing this you'll bring powerful energy to it. You can ask for a blessing on it when you're cooking it or simply say Grace when it's served.

- Food should be prepared with love.
- When you're eating, it's good to focus on your food and the people around you rather than TV, a mobile phone, or some other device. Instead appreciate the importance of your meal.

- Processed ready meals lack some of the powerful energies.
- Organic ingredients are a bonus.

If you still wonder what value is in a blessing. This was made so clear to me in the next memory I'm sharing with you.

Personally Speaking, early in my spiritual journey I visited the Harry Edwards Healing Sanctuary and attended some of the many talks they put on.

One particularly interested me. The subject concerned the basic energy value of food, and as an example we were shown auric photo slides of bread. The first slice was from a cheap supermarket loaf, and it had a faint glow of energy. The second was a wholemeal slice and that was much brighter. But the third slice, which was also wholemeal, was alive with energy. It shone very brightly because it had been blessed!

Honour Your Food

There's an aura around everything that has come from a living base or has passed through your energy when you used it. Simply by asking for a blessing on your food before you eat it or even when you prepare it you'll enhance its energy value. Combine that with a balance of colourful ingredients and you bring a bonus of nutritional energies to your meals.

If you're in a coffee shop or fast-food outlet, and you don't want to draw attention to yourself, then simply place your hand over the food, and silently ask God to bless it for you. When you choose a restaurant, pick one where the chef isn't bad tempered, and there's a happy mood. No one wants stressed food delivered to their table. This applies if the chef is male or female.

Where possible avoid processed readymade meals that may be produced by unenthusiastic operators working on a conveyor belt. Whether you're cooking for your family or for a soup kitchen, ask for a blessing to be given. I assure you that it works.

Protect Yourself

As a giving person who cares about others, your aura can reach out further than other people's. It's something that you'll notice in a queue when someone stands too close to you, and it feels uncomfortable. Also you can find that at times people leech off you, especially if you're a giver and they're a taker. They drain your energy. They may be dominant and like to use others for their own purposes, but give nothing back. I'm sure you know a few who fit that description. Some aren't even aware they're doing it.

But don't worry because it's a situation you can prepare for.

Find somewhere quiet to sit, close your eyes and envisage a pink bubble of love enveloping you. Enjoy the freedom and calm that it brings, and get on with your day.

If you have difficulty seeing the colour, find something that is that gentle shade of a rose quartz and focus on it. Draw the colour over you like a blanket so that it envelops you completely. It'll do the job just as well.

Love Unconditionally

I can't imagine a life without love. It's a special power that inspires us. God's Love empowers us and gets us through difficulties we don't always think we can handle.

As humans we often give our love selectively, and I don't just mean the love between life partners or families. We may select consciously or unconsciously whether someone should be given love. For instance, we will send our healing love to a victim, but the one who caused the pain is seen as undeserving.

However, unconditional love is for everyone. You don't have to like them first for them to go on your list. Just think… if you keep sending healing love *only* to the victims, there will simply be more victims. The perpetrator also needs your unconditional loving healing power otherwise they will continue to bring harm to others. So, ***don't*** be selective and ***don't*** judge.

That miserable looking neighbour that you avoid may need your love to brighten his day. You don't know what he's going through.

Send out your love unconditionally and ask God to use it where it's needed in the world. The more of us who do, the greater the impact.

Reawaken Your Instincts

Your instincts are a natural tool you have within you, and what you must do is ***choose*** to use them, because when you do, you react better to life. They're part of the equipment that God gave you, so don't overlook them:

1. Your sense of good, tells you 'you need to do this', even though you've no experience in it.
2. Your feeling of disquiet will tell you if something's not right.
3. There's also the feeling that says, 'This person's saying all the right things, but I don't feel comfortable about them.' Heed that too.

Your mind will offer you many ideas and yet when you focus on your senses, they can be very clear, so when you're directed in a particular way, don't ask 'why?' ask 'how?' and don't allow your second thoughts to push you off track. They're from your mind as it kicks in, and comes up with all its logical arguments for you to stay secure and bored in your comfort zone and therefore stop you from advancing. The go-getter is your soul, so go and get!

You'll gradually learn to recognise the **soul's** feelings within **you,** as they're the ones that make you feel good or bad about something, and they signal first.

Guidance and Healing Cards.

You may ask, 'How can cards help me? The answer is that God has a team of helpers there for everyone who asks, and when you choose a card, it's your choice of communication. It may be random, or you may subconsciously be looking for some guidance or reassurance, and the cards act as a tool through which these helpers can communicate with you. You're guided to the answers that are appropriate to you.

Personally Speaking, A few years ago, I remember giving a talk about guidance at one particular Mind Body Spirit Fair and there were 49 people in the audience. The previous day I had prepared 50 small sheets of paper with a piece of guidance. There were 5 specific areas of support. They were all folded and shuffled so there was a mix. At the beginning of my talk, I gave out the papers and later each person opened the one they had chosen. They all agreed that the guidance applied to them and found it surprising but helpful. I pointed out that although I didn't know the people in the audience, that God's helpers did, and as well as guiding me on what to write on the notes, they ensured that each person picked their appropriate paper.

As everyone left at the end, a lady came up to me and asked for a paper. She'd come in later in the talk. I had one left, and yes, it had an appropriate message.

There are many different tools that you can use to bring a lift to your day and also enhance your awareness, but guidance / healing / oracle cards are readily available from bookshops, new age shops and online, and they're a powerful tool. When you use them just ask for a blessing on them so that they work for *you*, and not the last person who handled them.

My own published sets are Woodland Wisdom Oracle Cards (artist Peter Pracownik). Jesus was my guide and instructed me with the messages They're now out of print and probably only available second-hand), Inspirational Wisdom from Angels and Fairies (artist Judy Mastrangelo) was the second, and the latest set Joyful Inspiration, again with Judy's beautiful paintings was a third requested by the publisher. They're all published by U.S Games in the U.S.A and are available worldwide in shops and online.

Added to these are many tarot cards, runes, and countless other types of guidance and healing cards. Just see what you're drawn to, and you'll find the right tools to suit your energies and your needs.

Be Positively Powerful

Every day is a new beginning, so don't automatically expect things to go wrong. Instead be positive.

You can be your own worst enemy if you allow yourself to disbelieve your power so ignore anyone around you who dismisses your efforts. It may take determination but ask God to help you. If days are challenging, do your best and focus on what you've achieved, rather than what you missed. Ask for God's Power and that will help you to succeed more.

The truth is that the way you think and speak influences your day, as well as the people around you, so inspire them with your positivity.

Don't worry *in case* something bad happens, it's time enough to worry if it does. Instead, be positive and help good to happen. Give it a reason to visit you, after all The Law of Attraction does work, and you don't want to encourage bad.

By this time, I would hope that you're gaining a sense of positivity, because the world needs that, as does God.

Just be aware of where your thoughts take you, and, at the beginning, be doubly cautious about what words you use.

Every time you fail takes you a step closer to success. Remember Thomas Edison said that he'd not failed, he'd simply found 10,000 ways that didn't work. Then he had that Lightbulb moment.

How many times did you hear a celebrity was an overnight success, and later that they'd struggled for a long time before. The truth is that many people work long and hard to fulfil their dreams, but then they appreciate more their success when it eventually comes.

And miracles do happen.

Personally Speaking, when I talk about miracles, one particular memory comes to mind. It was when my husband, Mike had a cataract in one eye. He was in his late 40s, and the specialist put him on the list for an operation with a year and a half wait. The problem was that he was a manager for an engineering firm and drove around 60,000 miles a year. He was already quite blind in that eye, so we searched and found a private clinic that would do the operation for around £1000, but that was our total savings at that time. The operation was essential for Mike's safety, so we paid, and within a fortnight it was done and successful. That same week we received a repayment for something in the past, which we had given up on. It was just £20 short of the amount we paid to the clinic, and it went straight back into our savings.

Remember that if your day has been turbulent, and you talk about it in a negative way, it will make it worse rather than better. So become upbeat and give the future the space to come right.

God has even given me pointers with some of my own prayers; so that I should say certain ones in a loving way and others with power and confidence.

Let words, as well as the way you express them, inspire you to open up to a life of positivity. Take time to listen to the magical quality of anyone who inspires, no matter who. It may even be you! Surprise yourself.

Finally, consider God's Words here:

'*Accept that what you have been given to do is a measure of your capability.*' In other words, ... '*You can do this!*' Now, that's inspiring and positive. So, if you need to ask something, don't ask, 'Why?' Ask 'How?'

Empower With Words

Positively change the way you speak to others. Tell them how they can succeed instead of how they may fail. You could be the life changer for others because words are a powerful tool and can inspire or crush.

There's so much inspiration in words spoken by people who've walked this life before us, and even some who share this time now. They can lift your day and strengthen your resolve as you strive towards your goal. Let them play a positive part in your future success.

Remember that words can inspire you or degrade you. They can fire your imagination or cripple it. They can bring peace, or start wars.

Let Others' Words Inspire You

Many famous names have given us beautiful and insightful statements that, at the right moment, can lift and dynamise us. But don't let the identity of the author decide the value of the saying. Just remember that Jesus once told me that many are so interested in the messenger they don't listen to the message. Instead we should allow the words to be the catalyst that inspires our journey.

Consider These Sayings

Martin Luther King Jnr: *'Only in the darkness can you see the stars.'* That's so true, sometimes we must reach the bottom before we can find a better way up.

Nelson Mandela: *'Do not judge me by my successes, judge me by the number of times I fell and got back up again.'* Yes, our failures can teach us the strength needed to become a success. So, forgive them and leave them behind.

Mother Teresa: *'If you do something out of duty it will deplete you, but if you do something out of love it will energise you.'* Put your heart into what you do, and it will excite you.

Gandhi: *'An eye for an eye only ends up making the whole world blind.'* I think this is a lesson that many people need to understand. Forgiveness *is* sweeter than revenge.

Lao Tsu: 'The journey of a thousand miles begins with one step.' It's being brave enough to take that first one.

Albert Einstein: *'Try not to be a man of success but rather try to be one of value.'* That's so important because value is now often counted in currency and that cannot value life.

Bruce Lee: *'Knowing is not enough, we must apply. Willing is not enough, we must do!'* So true. It's just what this book is about.

These wonderful words each carry their message and if you allow them they can inspire you to excel. Allow them to be the catalyst that will help you to get up when you fall, lick your wounds, and start again stronger.

My Personal Favourite

The following words from Mother Teresa are such a favourite of mine, and I have a framed copy that I keep by my desk. I believe the words offer a wonderful guideline for your life, and they have certainly been an inspiration to me:

Be the Light that You Are
People are often unreasonable, illogical, and self-centred.
Forgive them anyway.
If you are kind, people may accuse you of selfish motives.
Be kind anyway.
If you are successful, you will win some false friends and some true enemies.
Succeed anyway.
If you are honest, people may cheat you.
Be honest anyway.
What you spend years building, someone could destroy overnight.
Build anyway.
The good you do today, people will quite often forget tomorrow.
Do good anyway.
Give the world the best you have, and it may never be enough.
Give the world the best you've got anyway.
You see, in the final analysis, it is between you and God. It was never between you and 'them' anyway.

There are so many enriching words. Don't discard any simply because the writer is the wrong religion, from the wrong country, a different age, is the wrong sex or fails your judgement for one of many other reasons. Instead of prejudging, just listen to the words. Let them fuel your day with the dynamics they offer.

Other Aspects of Word Power

Never underestimate the potential effect of your own words either, for your emotion is transmitted through energy.

A few years ago, Dr Masaru Emoto did an interesting experiment with rice in jars, where he subjected it to different emotions from loving to hateful and he ignored some altogether. It was videoed and put on YouTube. The effect on the rice was astounding over one month and shows absolutely the result of negative emotions. So be aware of the power of words, for when you think or speak you do create energies. That's why prayer is so effective.

Your Special Time
Find at least a small part of your day for *you*. Do something that pleases and rewards you. Maybe you like to read, have time in the garden, walk, drive, watch films, knit, sew, listen to music etc. You deserve a little part of the day for your own needs, and it will help you to feel more worthwhile, and empower you for the more difficult times.

Be Tolerant
Although everyone is basically equal, their life lessons are probably different to yours, so instead of judging people, judge situations, and if they're wrong, help to improve them. Criticism is an empty comment unless you are prepared to follow it up with appropriate changes. Intolerance can blind everyone at times. So, ask for forgiveness when that happens to you.

Heal Yourself
This is a day-to-day technique to use when you need it.

Everyone is capable of healing; it's simply a personal choice whether to use it. Think of those times when children fall and hurt themselves, instinctively their mothers cover the sore area with their hands. It's a natural reaction and one that we can use on ourselves.

You can use your healing hands to diminish pain within your body. A woman with menstrual pain may clasp her hands around her abdomen and it's comforting. You do the same if you have a bad stomach, and a hand on your head helps with a headache.

You can hold your hands tight against the skin, or lift them an inch or so away, so you're healing through your aura. You may feel a buzz of energy, and the pain diminishing. If you have a clear, snow or rose quartz hold it with the fingers of the hand with which you give yourself healing. Whichever way you do it; ask God for help. As with so much, practice makes perfect, so use it regularly and God's Helpers will guide you to strengthen your healing ability.

Use this prayer:

'Dear Heavenly Power, please help me to ease the pain in my (name the area that's painful). Help me to feel some relief. I ask this in the knowing of God's Love given. Amen.'

You may find that you also need a cold / warm drink, to sit down for a while in the fresh air, lie down, or close your eyes. Act on it. Closing your eyes can be helpful as you can focus on the part you're healing, and if you follow your feelings you'll help yourself to heal quicker.

If you're in pain more regularly, then a visit to the doctor may be necessary. Guidance may have already pointed you in that direction, and if it has, don't ignore it.

Use Kindness

You can be selectively kind, or you can use that power for a wider good. Look for something that you can also do to help, which is outside the well-known choices. What do I mean? Well, you may be generous to the much-needed cancer charities or cat's and dog's homes, but how about that homeless person you pass outside the shopping mall. Why not make the effort and pop into the market and buy them some fruit, or a pastry and a drink from the local café? The gratitude on their face will cheer your day. Step outside your normal routine and it'll make you feel good!

Tools To Relax You
Music.

Use music as a wind down. Everyone needs to escape at times, and it can be therapeutic. There's a lot of stress in today's competitive world, and there are different genres of music to suit every mood or circumstance. They can soothe you, exhilarate you, and even empower you. So, allow it to heal you. If it annoys others, get a pair of headphones but don't be defeated.

God's Love.

Always remember that God's Loving Energy is there to empower you. If you find yourself in a position of conflict, you may want to flare up in response but both mentally and physically it takes its toll. A more powerful route is to back away and find a peaceful resolution, and God's Love is there to power you up to do that. It also gives you the strength to resolve other issues with love. Why not make up a small symbol and put it on every envelope you post, even the cheques for the taxman. Send your love with every communication. I do.

Guided Meditation.

A guided meditation CD can be an invaluable tool as it offers you some quality relaxation. There are many of these marketed now.

If you really want to get involved deeper with meditation and the guidance and awareness that can develop from it, look for an open meditation group in your area. It's empowering.

Relax And Release Fatigue

It's important to relax your mind and body at times for when you switch off your brain from the business of the day, you allow it space to take on vital guidance and inspiration. That allows your day to flow better, so that you achieve more. It's so easy to overwork your mind and body. We all do it. Just a little longer on the computer, or a few more hours of manual work, and we think it'll make a difference. No, actually taking some time to relax will make a difference! So, find somewhere quiet for yourself, and then allow God and His Team to access you. (Don't feel embarrassed if you're in the toilet or the bathroom, they're working with your spirit rather than your body, so if that's your quiet place, that's fine).

God needs you to rest at times, because He can't bring the valuable power updates that will help you to work smarter if you're so tired you can't recognise up from down. To be aware of new ideas and those inspired thoughts, you need to feel relaxed, so that there are no barriers to what's being given.

If you really ***need*** to move on, you have to grab calm breaks in your busy day. The more you do the faster you'll find yourself developing the life that you yearn for.

The Five-Minute Refresher

Everyone needs a break. It may be that at times work or a home situation is getting you down. There can be many reasons.

Here's a very simple Five-Minute Mind Relaxation that can help:
1. Take your lunch break and find somewhere where you won't be disturbed for five minutes.
2. Sit quietly and relax your body.
3. Roll your shoulders in a circular movement.
4. Gently rotate your head and neck so that the muscles relax in the top part of your body.
5. Shake your arms and hands to loosen any tautness.

6. Then close your eyes and breathe in deeply three or four times, each time holding the breath for a few moments before releasing.

As you feel calmer and more relaxed, take your mind back to a special time and situation where you laughed readily or maybe felt really happy and relaxed. Maybe it was on a beach..... if so, relive the feeling of the sand between your toes, and the water splashing over your feet as you stand gazing out to sea. The breeze is on your face, and you can smell the surf.

If it's a walk through the forest, smell the scent of the trees and the undergrowth; listen for the birds and the rushing stream while last year's golden leaves crunch under your feet.

Whatever your personal memory is, bathe in it for 3 to 4 minutes, and let yourself **re-live** the mood and the joy that you felt. Allow it to refresh you with sweet memories, before you return to the business of the day revived.

Prayers
What's In A Prayer?
God has guided me to say my prayers with feeling. That means showing my power and confidence as well as illustrating better my honest need and love. I found that difficult with religious prayers, but the ones I've included in this book were given to me by God and they're simple to say.

We can sometimes see prayers as a job we must get done. But when we speak those words with meaning, the prayer comes to life and the energy that it produces attracts the appropriate response.

Speaking Personally, I find that prayer is a wonderfully effective tool with which we can talk directly to God, and I have known clear results in both those prayers I've used for myself, and those that I have given others to use.

One occasion, a client came to me in a very distressed state. She was an Eastern European lady who'd been married for 25 years and had a very close relationship with her husband, but he had suddenly switched off. He'd turned cold towards her for no obvious reason.

I asked God for a prayer for her to say, and feeling a little comforted after her session with me, she went home. Two days later she called to say that she had said the prayer and within that short time things had returned to normal.

Put Together A Prayer

God has given me prayers to use for both my work and my personal needs, and it's taught me a lot about their construction. There are certain points that I've noticed about them that differ so much from some religious based prayers that I've said in the past.

- The language is clearer.
- The prayer frequently includes some sort of affirmation, which also offers me reassurance and helps me to realise or accept things.
- It often begins with a statement like, 'I am ready to believe' and 'I'm ready to move on.'
- Unsurprisingly, a prayer should be said in a respectful way.
- The way I say it makes a difference in the power of the prayer. Where needed, it's a plea for help, or a reassurance to God of my love, and a call for empowerment, and where appropriate it shows a feeling of abundance.
- The prayer should end with 'Amen' or 'So be it'.

So that's my own interpretation of some of the prayers God has given me. But I have also included in this section, a selection of prayers for you to use and maybe add to.

An Important Service of Clearance at the End of Your Life on Earth

We each carry painful or controlling negative energies within our soul when we die, but because they're from the Earth plane, they cannot be released in the Spirit Realms. As a result they stay with us and may influence our next life on Earth, blocking areas of our development and bringing unwanted difficulties. So, I asked God if there should be a service at the time of our passing that would release them.

Jesus had already told me that the Catholic Last Rites did this but had added that at times they were not given fully.

Also, to my knowledge, some other religions don't administer any version of the Last Rites, which I felt left us open to unwelcome challenges and blockages. Because of this I felt that some sort of release was vitally important.

God's answer was, "I feel now that there *is* a need for a more formal approach to death that allows the person, who is dying, to release failure, and employ a way of power through learning from it. So, I advise that a way forward should be given that is of this approach. This can be done with prayer.

He finished by saying,

"If this is given as a whole, they will feel restored by passing. Yet, at their death, if they are so weak bodily that they cannot ask for this themselves, someone who is ordained may ask for them."

So, to finish let me say that this short service prior to death as well as the other prayers are here for you to use as you need.

Here is a small selection of prayers for different occasions.

I thank members of our Love Worldwide Prayer Group for some of them, as God gave me the words in response to their requests.

Personal Prayers

Food Pre-Death Release
Dear Heavenly Power,

I ask to release from within me all the sins and upsets that I have committed.

I ask to bring forward a need for growth.

I ask for forgiveness for all parts of my life, and for the development that has seen prowess without reward, and for all upset throughout.

I ask for forgiveness for others, who have affected my life with sin.

I ask forgiveness for my soul.

I ask this of God, whom I trust. Amen.

A Blessing For Your Food
Say this while you're preparing food or just before eating it.

I ask for a blessing on this food. Amen.

Alternatively, before you eat.

Grace: For what we're about to receive, may the Lord make us truly thankful. Amen.

Forgiveness
Daily Forgiveness
I forgive myself and I seek forgiveness.

I hold within the power to forgive, and I open my heart to

forgive with every breath I take. I do this in God's knowing.

Amen.

Self-Forgiveness
I ask Dear Heavenly Power, to be forgiven for my actions and any hurt brought.

Allow me the peace of knowing that I am forgiven, and help me too to forgive.

For the strength and power that is given by God shall enable me to then move on as a result.

Amen

Forgiveness Exercise

I ask now, Dear Heavenly Power,

for forgiveness to enter my soul, so that I may move on in my life,

and not stay entrenched in hate or self-loathing.

I ask for forgiveness for my own part in those issues where I have caused hurt,

and I ask for forgiveness to be given to all those who have caused me pain.

I know that I no longer need to carry the anger and upset within me,

as it is detrimental to my health, and to the power I carry that is given by God.

Let it be that I learn from this experience,

and never again fear the need to release all anger and pain within me,

so that I may move on in my life. I ask this of God in whom I trust.

Amen.

Personal Development
Empowerment

Dear Heavenly Power I ask for the will to do what is right for my life at this comples time

Let me feel the wisdom and power that God gives, so that I may remove the barriers of upset from my mind and see instead, a powerful way forward of endurance and active change.

Let me be wiser for it to able to balance my life better,

and let me not seek the upset of unrealistic thinking,

but allow myself to be led by my heart and purpose to do good, not

only in my need to move on, but also that of others too.

I ask this in the knowing of God's Love given.

Amen.

Personal Development

I need now, Dear Heavenly Power, to move forward and develop.

I ask for both help and guidance in this.

Amen.

Moving Forward

I am ready now to impart a value within my soul that activates a need for soul cleansing.

For I am rid of that active and worthwhile structure that can illuminate my life,

and so, my life is stagnant as a result, and it may be painful at those times,

where I stretch myself to take in more worth and yet fail.

So, I ask now for the willingness of God's Soul to enter mine,

and reunite me with the pleasantness and worth I need,

for the way forward to be of true balance to me.

Amen.

Self-Assurance
Reassurance

I ask now to the Power of God, for a way forward tha t allows me to plan

in a better and more powerful way for a stable result.

Let it be that I am given a way forward of true power, by devising a way of true balance; so that I may achieve my goals in full, and relieve my way of the upset of not k

nowing,
if I am capable of completing my journey of worth in full.

Let it be that I am at one with myself. I ask this in the knowing of God's Power given.

Amen.

Staying Positive
I ask, Dear God,

for this day to shape up in the best possible way, so that I may learn and feel joy throughout.

I ask that I am given the power to do my tasks, and to realise that even if I fail, I am still learning. I ask now for the wisdom and power to be given that will keep me positive.

Amen.

Coping With Personal Difficulties
Coping at a Difficult Time (Given during Covid Lockdown)

Dear Heavenly Power, I ask for the will to do what is right for my life at this complex time.

Let me feel the wisdom and power that God gives, so that I may remove the barriers of upset from my mind and see instead a powerful way forward of endurance and active change.

Let me be wiser for it to be able to balance my life better and let me not seek the upset of unreal thinking but allow myself to be led by my heart and purpose to do good, not only in my need to move on, but that of others too.

Amen.

Those Feeling Suicidal
For Those Who Feel Suicidal

I ask, dear Heavenly Power, that the factors that cause someone to take their own life abate, and that they take back the need to feel suicidal and breathe in again the air of a living person, who has the power and endurance to resist the mental capacity that vents danger.

Let them bring instead a new Light, a beginning to their lives that contemplates good.

For the withering thoughts of a mind that is in danger of suicide can overtake that empowerment the soul brings to endure and feel the power surge of God.

Let that of Thy Wisdom prevail, that they may counteract the turbulence within, and gain power again as a soul filled by love.

Amen.

Children
For All Children In Need

I ask now for empowerment to be given to all those children, who need help in their lives.

I am ready to believe that the wisdom and value given by God, shall incorporate the empowerment needed, for all children to feel embraced by love and valued in full.

Let them learn the wisdom of love and correct any imbalances that do not allow their way forward to be blessed. I ask this of God whom I love and trust fully.

Amen.

Healing
Healing Yourself And Others

I am ready now to bring forward a healing power of strength to change lives. Let it be that I am the factor of
change that allows this to happen.

I ask now for help to be given especially to the following people…. (Speak the names).
Amen

Hands On Self-Healing

'Dear Heavenly Power, please help me to ease the pain in my… (name the area that is painful).

Help me to feel some relief. I ask this in the knowing of God's Love given.

Amen.'

Spiritual Growth And The Healing Of Humanity

I ask now, dear Heavenly Power for a structure so great that we can bring forward the growth of humanity to a better basis, and one where it stands tall in its dominion and proudly says, 'We are at one in our deliberations, and our functions grow as we work together.'

Let it be for this reason that the world responds to humanity's needs, and fulfils its pledge to the Earth, and all those who live upon it.

Let it be that we bring the Divine Power of God, for the future to be blessed and open to change of the best kind.

Amen.

Natural Disasters

I ask now for those, who have suffered and lost in the recent disaster to be comforted and held close to God.

I ask this so that the wherewithal of those helping to salvage lives and property can hold fast, and be of service to their own safety, as well as the ones who have died, or been made homeless by such upsetting circumstances.

Guide them and bring them the strength and love needed to do what is vital to all at such a time.

Amen.

Peace

I ask Dear Heavenly Power, for power to be given to the peacemakers,
such that they will bring a force of good to the world again.
I ask that where there is brutality within the world,
it will be displaced by love of an empowering nature,
so that we may breathe together in the empowering force of love given by God.
I ask this of God whom I trust.
Amen.

Terrorism
End Terrorism

I am given now to ask for a simple matter of terror to bring less upset to the world,
for it has pursued a career of upsetting proportions through the efforts
of those who create mayhem through a love of evil.
For they're not displaying God's Love, and it's a hopeless task to expect
a man to feel at ease with the need for a weapon in his hand.
Yet he has the option to put it down and walk away.
I ask now that he finds the need to resist all anger,
and to use the power within as a basis for love instead.
Amen.

For Those Injured Through Terrorism

I ask for now the wisdom and power of healing to be given to all those,
who succumb to the pain and terror of terrorists.
Let them be vitalised by God's love and find their way forth.

through the bombardment of hate and upset within them
to a legacy of love and a creative force for peace.

Let those who are blown apart by the upset of this crisis,
be put together by God's Love and create a force so great.
that we can unite the world through love and not war.
Amen.

For The Souls Of Those Killed Through Terrorism

I pray for the souls of those departed through the rage and upset of a terrorist,
and I ask now that they pass through the healing and wisdom of God's Love
to bring forward a new journey of love again in the Spirit Realms.
Amen.

The World and Planet Earth
Planet Earth

I am ready to believe that I can contribute to the health of the Earth through my prayers.

I ask for this to happen, and for the way forward to be based on a new and more powerful
phase of life, in order to bring about a calmer energy to its core, and a vibrancy to its future
overall. I ask this in the name of all good.
Amen.

Repair The World And Its Oceans

I am ready now to accept that the past failures have shown an ill kept worth for the world in all its needs.

Where it has shown love, the world has been rewarded by hate or an incompetence that has shown least value for the world, and more for the worth of mankind.

Let it be now that we take forward the love given by God, and use it to impair no longer the needs of the world and this planet, but to unfold a love so great that we shall take forward our ability to repair the oceans and the life within.

Let it be that we take forward the forest and the blessings of life so often discarded,

and value the rivers and tributaries for what they are, a basis of life for all that is good, and not to be poisoned by mankind's need for control in an unhappy and tormented way.

Let it be that we are blessed by a more rapid change of formula

that allows growth to be renewed, and mankind's deprivation to be ended.

I love this planet, and I need now to heal what is rotten, take away the harm, the bruising choices we make, and value the whole once more in the Light of God.

Amen.

Prayers For Animals
Animals Also Have Souls

Just as the soul is an integral part of a human being, it's also a basic part of all animals, and it allows them to carry certain beneficial understanding within, so that their lives can become clear to them.

Knowledge such as feeding, and reproducing are a basic understanding that any animal's brain would not tell them, but their soul will, because it has a memory of everything before this life, whereas the brain relies purely on experiences within this life to teach it and guide its decisions.

Yet, while the soul-based instincts can deliver the understanding to a lion to chase down its prey, it also inspires a gazelle to use speed and its natural manoeuvrability to avoid being caught.

Their instincts deliver the understanding of a hierarchy which exists within the animal kingdom. However, that doesn't allow for the unpredictable thinking of humankind, who imagines that he already understands the needs and abilities of all animals and interferes in ways that he shouldn't.

Just as humans live many lives on Earth, so do animals.

Many have known abuse and cruelty in previous lives, as well as this one, and they carry the memory. But as humans we can help them cut loose from those negative energies when they pass from this life, by using the relevant prayers for their soul. It will free them, and it's the last act of kindness that you can perform for any animal, whether they die at home or elsewhere.

Personally Speaking, an example of that was in August 2022 when my rescued canine friend, Buzz died of pancreatic cancer. We had shared just seven years when he died.

At the end of his life, our Spanish vet had to help him to pass, but he waited quietly at the side while I said two prayers for my special friend, who passed peacefully. My Spirit Guide, Abuhindra assured me that we had performed the kindest act as he was in pain, and he confirmed that his spirit had made the journey safely.

Selection Of Prayers For Animals
Prayer For A Sick Animal

I ask God in the knowing of all good, to bring about a rational ability to heal (name) 's ills.

Allow him to feel the basis of our love, and know that we're at one with his need to recover and bring about good health for him.

Allow him to construct a powerful way of rebuilding his constitution so that he may not wither but instead return to a good and mighty future with us in full.

I ask this of God in whom I trust.

Amen.

Healing Past Lives

(Say this with love)

I ask for help for this animal. I ask forgiveness for the pathway that brought it pain.

I bring forgiveness in my heart, and I breathe that which is forgiving into the heart of this animal. Let it be healed.

Amen.

For Animals Generally

I am ready now to believe in the wisdom of coveting our animal kingdom,

in a way where they can be vitalised and empowered to bring a valuable worth to the world.

For they are abused and threatened in so many ways that it's become a fragile power within the world.

Yet, we may see improvement to the world itself, if we hold true to the need to care for,

and not abuse the animals so precious to us; for we are the ones that hold such power,

and it shall be to us that the world holds resentment, if we abandon the need to bring life, and not abuse to our animals. I ask this in the knowing of God's Love given.

Amen.

To Protect Animals

There are many ways, Dear Heavenly Power where the human race is abusing and torturing animals, and there is no discretion whether it be a wild animal or a tame one.

We ask now that those, who are of a mind to use ways of torture or neglect

to abuse and hamper the lives of so many animals, are given a need to forfeit their way of destruction and use their power to bring about a change of heart, and a determined direction of conservation. Let those who require it feel the punishment of the law

and allow those who require a need of solidarity against harming animals to

be given strength and the funds needed, to continue their work. We ask this in God's Name.

Amen.

To End Abuse Of Animals (incl Dogs in Meat Trade)

I am aware of the worth and value of all animals, whether within society's base or the wilderness beyond our towns and cities.

Please Lord God, let it be that the astonishing cruelty has a base no more in mankind's thinking,

as there is a need now for the wisdom of mankind to evaluate his principles as a whole,

and realise that we are wearying the bond between us, and the animals that we so readily abuse in whatever form, whether it be for their fur, food or just for cruelty's sake.

Let us take this abysmal abuse and make it extinct, before we realise that the whole of the kingdom of animals is beyond our reach, and no longer available to us in whatever our needs.

Let us feel the joy of hope, that once the power to protect animals is seen, and exercised throughout the world, we shall be worthy of them again, and never abuse that gift they bring us.

Amen.

End Of Life Prayers For Animals

Clearing Bad Energies from An Animal's Soul At The End Of Its Life on Earth (Like the Last Rites)

I bless and hold in true and valuable worth the soul of this animal that is to pass.

I fully know of its ills, and the pain suffered.

I know of the fear it holds from the past, and I ask forgiveness to bring a healthy soul to its timed passing, from the life it now holds to the life ahead in spirit.

I do this as I ask for protection to be given.

In the Name of our Lord God.

Amen.

For an animal's soul to pass easily to its spirit home use this next prayer.

For The Soul Of An Animal

I ask for this hallowed creature's soul to pass willingly, and with love to its future home in the Spirit Realms.

I ask for the healing of its soul, so, no suffering follows.

In the Name of our Lord God.

Amen.

If you want to pray daily for the souls of animals that die daily through slaughterhouses, science laboratories, bull fighting rings, etc. use this prayer.

For the Souls of Many Animals

I ask for the hallowed creatures' souls in (slaughterhouses, science laboratories, bull fighting rings) to pass willingly, and with love to their future home in the Spirit Realms.

I ask for the healing of their souls, so no suffering follows. In the Name of our Lord God.

Amen.

Finally, we may fear that we won't meet our pets again after their time on Earth is over, but we do. They live on.

I have had the joy of meeting two of our dogs after they moved to spirit. It was on an occasion when I couldn't sleep because of pain, and they came to bring healing. I even stroked one of them and he felt just the same.

So never fear that they've gone. They're just nearby, waiting.

Frances Munro Bio

Life's been Frances' teacher, and with God's help she's gained a rounded education. Attending a private girls' school, she then trained as a mechanic in her father's racing car garage.

Her mother was a narcissistic alcoholic for over 40 years, and life was challenging both as daughter and carer. Spiritualism and healing turned her hurt into tolerance and compassion.

She's married to Mike Munro and has an adult son.

In 1998, Frances qualified as spiritual healer and developed her spiritual awareness. Later, she started receiving guidance from her Apache spirit guide, White Cloud, who helped her believe in her ability. In May 1999, Jesus took over, and gave her work a much wider focus, also explaining the presence of elementals, angels, and the roles of Satan, Lucifer, and the Devil.

He introduced her to the practicality of God's needs and guided her to work with offenders. She counselled a lifer in prison and volunteered with the Probation Services. The challenge taught her about areas of life, of which she had no understanding. In 2001, he guided her small spiritual group to help in the world by sponsoring a child in a needy country. From that grew a charity called Give Youth A Hand, run completely by volunteers.

They helped homeless centres and women's refuges in England. Frances' home became Head Office, storage, and packing station. They sponsored 11 children, and then, after the Balkans War, began delivering aid first to homeless centres, hospitals, schools, and children's homes in Croatia, and the Red Cross in Serbia. She and Mike took aid twice a year, at times organising convoys of up to 30 vehicles. Between visits they raised funds and arranged deliveries of furniture, and equipment.

In 2011 Jesus told her to receive God's messages, as well as those of Esquaygo, an extraterrestrial. Meanwhile, her life changing courses, retreats, talks, and regression sessions had become popular, and work spread in the UK, Norway, Sweden, and California, USA. She also recorded a one-hour training video in Santa Monica for the Learning Annexe.

In 2015, God guided Mike and Frances to move to Spain which they did within 5 months, and now Frances focuses on writing and online work, developing a powerful following on Quora.

In 2017, God guided her to start a prayer group. The Love Worldwide Prayer Group now has 57 members in 9 countries.

She's a minister of the Universal Life Church, based in California.

In 2019, God told her to communicate with a powerful spirit guide called Abuhindra, whose focus is to help humankind bring changes to reverse the serious decline in this planet's strength and the abhorrent selfishness of humanity.

That communication continues.

Printed in Great Britain
by Amazon